Also by TONY STOLTZFUS

Leadership Coaching: The Disciplines, Skills and Heart of a Christian Coach

Coaching Questions: A Coach's Guide to Powerful Asking Skills

A Leader's Life Purpose Workbook

Christian Life Coaching Handbook

Peer Coach Training Facilitator's Guide

Peer Coach Training Workbook

The Calling Journey: Mapping the Stages of a Leader's Life Call

Questions for Jesus: Conversational Prayer Around Your Deepest Desires

The Invitation: Transforming the Heart Through Desire Fulfilled

To order copies of these books
and other materials by Tony Stoltzfus, visit
www.Coach22.com
or call 877-427-1645

TONY STOLTZFUS
with CHRIS FROST

Heaven's
PERSPECTIVE
STORIES FROM THE BOOK OF LIFE

HOW A GOOD GOD TRANSFORMS SUFFERING INTO GLORY

Preface

Since this book is made up of the life stories of others—stories they each paid a significant price to be able to tell—I'd like to thank all those who contributed their tales for helping to making this a great book. Your stories will be told and retold in heaven throughout eternity! I won't name you all here because many of you have elected to remain anonymous (usually in order to protect family and friends), but I am very grateful all the same.

I'd also like to thank our first storywriting team, who are helping to launch this to a wider audience: Chris Frost, who has launched our first Leadership MetaFormation affiliate site; Danielle Schmidt, our Event Coordinator (who has moved on to become a full-time intercessor); and Kathy Stoltzfus, the Director of Leadership MetaFormation (and my wife!).

Also, a big shout-out goes to Jesus, who is the behind-the-scenes author of all these stories and made all of this possible. Thanks for talking to us, thanks for revealing some of the surprises you have stored up for us in heaven, and thanks for being a true friend. We're very proud of you!

Table of CONTENTS

Introduction

*"The heart speaks the language of experience. To change
the heart, you must experience something different."*

Tony Stoltzfus

T his book was born out of a crazy idea I tried in a workshop
to help people recognize God's activity in their life stories.
Since the workshops are about touching the heart, each workshop begins with a "Taste of Heaven" experience—a heaven
simulation with audience participation. The room is wrapped
all around in white fabric, with staging, lighting, actors, dance,
original music, and more. Putting on a Taste of Heaven is a ton
of work, but it's incredibly powerful for the participants.

But this time my wife was wondering if I'd gone a little
overboard. For the *Living from the Heart* workshop I decided
to interview everyone who was coming about one of their most
painful experiences in life, rewrite each story from heaven's
perspective, and then present it in a hand-made, personalized

"Book of Life" when they were ushered into the heaven room. Wouldn't that be an awesome way to learn to see life from heaven's point of view?

It was a cool idea, but I hadn't fully considered what it would be like to listen to 30 people recount all the details of their most painful life experiences. To rewrite those stories through God's eyes, I had to engage their journeys deeply. At two hours per story, that was 60 hours of swimming in the bitterest depths of the human experience, comingled with witnessing the creative glory of Jesus' redemptive activity. I grieved with them, cried with them, and cried again when I wrote to them through the eyes of heaven. It was a bit emotionally draining, to say the least!

However, the impact of the stories was greater than I had imagined. The workshop participants often had huge, tearful breakthroughs in their relationships with God, or put doubts and questions to rest that had plagued them for years. Those stories got read over and over (some are still reading them!), like meat and drink for the soul.

The process changed me as well. During that first period of writing God-stories, I got into a mode where it seemed like I could ask Jesus any question I could think of about heaven and I'd get an answer (e.g. "Jesus, are there haircuts in heaven?"). Much of what he revealed made its way into that first set of stories, and into many later ones.

Since then, we've built a team of storywriters and created a set of tools for bringing heaven's perspective to any person's story. In this book we want to share some of the God-stories we've written with you.

Your STORY

You, too, have a God-story,[1] although you probably only know part of it. In this *Book of You* heaven is writing, your life finally makes sense. You are in a process of growth that, no matter your faults or failings, is relentlessly drawing you toward the heart of God. Your God-story is not about what you've accom-

---

1　*If you'd like to have your own story rewritten from heaven's perspective, or give the gift of a story to a friend, visit www.HeavensPerspective.com to sign up. Or attend our* Living from the Heart *workshop—the story is included in the workshop experience. Details are at www.Meta-Formation.com.*

plished or how you performed—it's a romance between a regular human and the Son of God who is madly in love with you. The tale it tells is that heaven is the real home of your heart and the happy ending that makes all things well.

You need to know your God-story, because reading it can lift the weight of suffering from your shoulders and bring your heart to life. And those around you need to know it, too—because when it is told from heaven's perspective, your story can change the world.

Chapter 1:
GETTING PERSPECTIVE

"And I saw the dead, great and small, standing before the
throne, and books were opened. Also another book was
opened, which is the book of life. And the dead were judged
by what was written in the books, by what they had done."

(Rev. 20:12 RSV)

The story of your life is being written down in heaven. Each
day a new page is penned in this *Book of You*, carefully prepared for that ultimate moment when it is read out in full before
the throne of God. But get ready for a jaw-dropping surprise
on the day you first hear heaven's story (Jesus loves surprises!),
because the way you remember your life is far different than
what is written about you in heaven. Your own memories are
like snapshots of a fading past, taken through the blurred lens of
earthly vision. Even your best memories are tinged with the brokenness and pain of humanity. But the *Book of You* wipes away
the dirt of earthly life and instead views you through the eyes of

a Good Father, your Creator. You will look on yourself through this lens of glory and see yourself just as he sees you—from heaven's perspective.

Reading THE BOOK OF YOU

What would it be like to settle into a comfortable chair with a cup of java, open heaven's book and absorb a God's-eye view of your life story? The first thing you'd notice is how much of your own tale you never knew. Instead of a hidden future of blank pages, you'd read right to the end of the *Book of You* and see how Jesus gloriously redeems all your fumbles and failures. Relationships you thought were irretrievably broken are somehow put better-than-right. Assignments you left unfinished in your time on earth miraculously appear in heaven fully completed—and fully rewarded. The redemption Jesus pulls off in your story is so utterly all-embracing that *every* word God spoke over you "will not return to [him] empty, but will… achieve the purpose for which [he] sent it" (Is. 55:11 NIV). Beyond hope, heaven has made all things well.

Flipping back toward the beginning of the book, you encounter whole chapters written before you were born, recounting how your Good Father arranged people and circumstances to bring you to life and shape you into the person he designed. The wonder of how he took the brokenness of those who came before you and used it to create the beauty of your destiny would leave you in awe. And each page of your history would be filled with Father's delight in little things long forgotten: a sunrise painted just for you, flowers blooming on your breakfast table, or a simple act of kindness worthy of an incredible eternal reward.

Another huge revelation would be the connections between your own destiny and the destinies of others. On earth, the only story you are truly familiar with is your own. But in the heaven's book you'll see deeply into how your calling is entwined with the destinies of hundreds of those around you, thousands who came before you, and generation upon generation of those who came after you. With astonishment, you'll perceive how every other life has touched yours, and fully understand how your life has touched all others. You'll know, to the same degree you've been fully known by your Father in heaven, the full impact of everything you've done. In that moment, every yearning you've ever felt for meaning and purpose in life will be filled to overflowing.

Each new insight from heaven will explode how you understand reality. For example, just reading a story written from a perspective outside of earth's time will be a mind-bender. On earth, you've lived trapped within time, chained to being present in just one moment, and then another, and then another. Time marches on, and you cannot change it or step out of it.

But time is not the master of eternity. Father is the great I AM, dwelling outside of created time, experiencing every individual moment of our time all at once. All of earth's history is swallowed up within his eternal now, so that all moments are this present moment to him. As you read the *Book of You* in Father's house, you are not recalling past events or looking forward to future times, but entering into and *living* each page now, present in each story you read. Heaven's books aren't a dead record of things past, but a living experience of what was and is and ever more shall be.

However, the best is yet to come. The most heart-stopping, worship-inducing shift will be experiencing how you impact the Author's heart. The *Book of You* doesn't merely recount the facts of what happened in your life. It is the record of the Author's thoughts toward you. When you see yourself through his eyes, you also get to actually *experience* Jesus' thoughts, emotions and desires as he watches your life unfold. You will step into the mind of Christ toward you and experience the tremendous pride he feels when he thinks of you. You'll be captivated by his deep longing to bring you home to him, and romanced by the intensity of his affections. Here on earth, you see him through a mirror dimly, even in your holiest moments grasping a mere sliver of his power, grace and extravagant love. In heaven, the full weight of his glory passes into your being as he shares his glory with you, transforming you forever. From that moment on, you will always, only see yourself as he sees you. Doubt and fear will die forever, and everything you ever desired will be yours, always.

Then your eyes open, and a flicker of disappointment grazes your heart as you peer around your familiar, darkened living room.

You are still in your old chair, a cold cup of coffee on the side table and a Bible in your lap, still waiting for a Kingdom that is yet to come. You haven't died and gone to heaven—you've just been given a fleeting taste of what's to come. Bummer.

A few deep breaths settle your racing heart, and you begin to make your peace with going back to normal life. But something is different. You suddenly realize that you actually brought a piece of heaven back with you. You have heaven's perspective. Until today, you've interpreted your life through the words of many voices: the voice of God, but also the disapproving words of your inner critic, the pain of your past wounds, the opinions of those around you, and your anxieties about the future. Until today, those voices have filled in much of the unknown in your story with dark doubts and nagging fears.

But now you've seen you through Jesus' eyes, and everything is illuminated by the light of heaven. You *know* the truth: that you are extravagantly loved by the only One that matters, and no failure or fear can pull you apart. Your Jesus is proud of you, satisfied with you, pleased as punch, and can hardly wait for you to come home to his house and read the rest of the God-story he's written just for you. He passionately longs for you to see him as he really is, in his glory, and for you to see yourself through his eyes.

Yes, you've seen heaven's perspective. You'll never look on life the same way again.

A Peek INTO HEAVEN

What would happen if you could read your own biography today—the one written through Jesus' eyes? Could it be possible to actually get a sneak peek at the *Book of You* hidden in heaven? I believe you can.

This book is about seventeen ordinary people who got the chance to read a page of their stories from the books of heaven. It wasn't just any page—the curtain was pulled back on one of their most painful experiences in life. In the midst of real tragedy and deep loss, they witnessed the Author of life writing their redemption story. He dipped his pen in his own blood, crossed out every line of pain and grief, and wrote in joy and glory instead.

These seventeen individuals read the final end of their story from the perspective of heaven. And they were transformed.

Kathy's journey (see chapter five) is a powerful example. Her life was turned upside down when her first child, Kait, was born severely autistic and severely mentally disabled. Now 24, Kait is happy and physically active, but never developed the ability to care for herself or even to speak. Kathy went from a productive, recognized leadership position at her church to 24 years of full-time care for just one person—a person who is largely unable to give back. Her story is one of beautiful service, but also of pain. "That's one of my deepest desires," Kathy related to me tearfully. "I'd just like to hear my daughter say the word, 'Momma.'"

But then heaven spoke. Kathy discovered how a good God took that meaningless suffering and employed it to deepen the love between her and her daughter, so their relationship in heaven would be deeper and more satisfying than it ever would have been had evil not tried to interfere. She saw redemption triumph over that physical disability, and understood how heaven would put all things better than right at the end. In heaven, Kathy will hear a lifetime's-worth of those words she's longed to hear, spoken by the daughter she has loved so well for so little in return.

"Having my story reframed from heaven's perspective was deeply impacting and life-altering," Kathy affirms. "My heart and head aligned. It left me feeling known, accepted and empowered."

The Power OF PERSPECTIVE

However, reading her story in heaven's book didn't change a single thing about Kathy's circumstances. Knowing the God-story doesn't alter your outward situation at all. So how can something be life-changing without bringing any concrete change to your life?

The past cannot change, but what *does* change is our perspective: what we believe about what happened. Changing the belief system we use to look at our history makes an enormous difference. As Natalie puts it, "I was so caught up in my 'wrong' decisions in my life that I couldn't see that God was with me in them. I saw him working his purpose for my life, but I still lived in the sense of right and wrong. But now I am free!"

I've coached hundreds of leaders through their most difficult moments in life, and I've come to an important conclusion:

Much of your pain (or peace) comes from your perspective.

What you believe alters what you experience. The death of your child is a terrible thing—that pain is real. But when you believe it is because God is punishing you, it hurts that much more. Losing a limb is painful physically and emotionally, but if you believe it makes you less of a person, that hurt will remain long after the physical pain fades. Getting fired from your job isn't fun, but when you are afraid it will mean losing everything you've worked so hard to save over the last 20 years, unemployment becomes that much more ominous.

But now look from a different perspective: what if you knew that two weeks from now you'd get a great job offer, for much more than you are making now? Or even better, what if you fully believed that leaving this position was the thing that would launch you into your destiny? Would things still seem so grim? No! In fact, you might even take a family vacation and *enjoy* your two weeks off instead of worrying the entire time.

Perspective is a powerful thing. And getting a window into how God sees your life unfolding can radically change how you experience your situation.

Learning THROUGH STORY

So how do we learn to see from heaven's perspective? New perspective means new beliefs. Our brains need to be rewired to believe differently about who God is and how he works in our lives. To displace the religious pictures of an angry, distant God we picked up along the way, we'll need to experience a Good Father who loves us lavishly and longs to be good to us.

Experience is the key. Our core beliefs form through experience, not rational thought or reading words on a page. *So to change our beliefs, we have to have different experiences.*

Let me demonstrate. Pick up a pen or pencil off your desk and hold it out in front of you. What will happen if you let go of it? We all know: it will fall to the ground due to the force of gravity. Okay, so here's the important question: where did you learn that? It wasn't in school. Scientists have discovered that babies understand that unsupported objects will fall at only a few months old. You learn about gravity by *experiencing* it. Only much later do you figure out how to explain what you've observed. In fact, one way to think about beliefs is that they are *the explanations we develop for our experiences.*

Our brains work the same way when it comes to God: what we believe is formed much more by our experiences than our theological explanations. For example, you may know about the love of God from reading Scripture, but still find yourself feeling afraid that he'll punish or reject you if you screw up. Your gut-level beliefs line up much more with how you experienced punishment and grace in the past than they do with what you've read.

Still don't believe me? Here's a great way to experience firsthand where beliefs come from. (Note: you have to actually put yourself into this and *do this exercise* to get the point.) First, think of an area of your life you are not proud of, something about you that needs to change, or a place where you feel you are really falling short. Jot it down below:

_____

Did you write something down? Good. The next step is to pray this prayer: "Father, send me the circumstances I need to change in this area." I'll give you a moment to do it.

The exercise here is not praying that prayer—it is observing what happens inside you when you are asked to do it. So, what emotions did you experience in that moment?

I've done this exercise repeatedly with groups of mature Christian leaders, and the near-universal reaction is fear—even panic or terror. Why? Because our interpretation of our past experiences (our belief) is this: "If I ask God to send me the circumstances I need to change, they'll be bad ones." In our head (our rational brains) we know God is good. It says so in scripture. However, the part of us that learns by experience (our emotional brains) believes the opposite. When the pressure is on, how we see God is determined more by our experiences (and what we believe about them) than by our Bible knowledge.

Since your beliefs are formed by experiences, they change when you have different experiences. So the best way to learn to see from heaven's perspective is to experience it in your own life. The next best way is to watch God at work in the lives of others. So let's dive into a story!

Cami is a friend and co-worker whose story is a good example of this perspective shift. Her tale (like all those in the book) is presented in three parts:

1. Cami's story of her painful experience seen through her own eyes.
2. The God-story, told by Jesus from heaven's perspective.
3. Finally, Cami's account of how experiencing heaven's perspective impacted her life.

As you absorb her story, pay attention to how God employs broken vessels to bring his wholeness into her life.

Cami's STORY

Meet Cami and you'll see that her happy, effervescent energy spills over all around her. You'd never know she spent the first several decades of her life under repressive communist rule in Romania. Gymnastics was her life until she was 14, when the State suddenly removed her coach and shut down the program, leaving her distraught and completely lost. It was the first of a series of traumatic incidents that led her to close her heart to God and other people, until she met the great heart-opener, Jesus.

"I grew up in an Orthodox church," Cami recalls. "I didn't know the loving God, only the God that would punish me if I did something wrong. I was afraid of him. That fear stayed in my life even after I immigrated to the United States in 2002.

"Six or seven years ago, a friend invited me to a charismatic church. I thought God would be pissed at me if I went—like I was betraying the God I knew by going to a different church—so I kept putting her off. She pursued me for years, just kept asking and asking, so I finally went just to get rid of her. They worshipped with hands up, singing and dancing. I had never seen anything like that in the Orthodox church, where everything was very strict and in the service nobody moved. Part of me wanted to run out of this strange, new place, but my spirit was extremely happy—something came alive inside me. So I kept going back. One Sunday someone preached about what it means to have Jesus in your heart, and I went up and rededicated my heart to Jesus. I had been running away from my emotions for years, but now I could not stop crying. I cried day and night for months. I still cry in worship to this day.

"But it was a long journey to that point of reopening my heart. After gymnastics ended I rebelled and ran away from home for several months. I married my first husband basically thinking of it as revenge toward my dad, to show him that he couldn't control me and I could do whatever I wanted.

"My second marriage started off better but got worse and worse over time. It was just after my first divorce. I was not attracted to him at first; he was attracted to me. He kept calling and calling. He called me every day when he was in the country. He was one of those guys that people are drawn to—he was very charismatic, very intelligent—and we could talk for hours. But I didn't really want to be with him. It wasn't love. I just had compassion for him because he was a train wreck.

"When we first met, the compassionate part of me kicked in as he talked about losing his mother. He had all these hurts from his dad, he didn't really have friends—he was grieving and I was his counselor. He kept saying that I was his medicine.

"Since I was hurt in the same way, it gave me someone to talk to as well. The way he reacted made me feel valued. I thought, 'I *am* good for something. I am good at something with guys. I'm not completely rejected.' Comforting him gave me comfort. With two wounded people… I guess my needs will get filled in one way or the other, in a healthy way or unhealthy way.

"We were together for eight years and married for three. After we got married in Romania, I came to the U.S. where he was living. When I got off the plane and saw him waiting, I thought, 'This is a stranger. What am I doing here?' Things went south from there.

"I discovered that he was having trouble with drugs. He was very good at hiding. These awful guys kept coming to collect money from me, and I got scared. There was a lot of threatening and intimidation—and I was paralyzed by fear. He threatened to write to Homeland Security and report me, and I didn't want to be in trouble with the government. I kept having to call 9-1-1 about him yelling and fighting and throwing stuff. Finally, I mustered up the guts to talk to an attorney about filing for divorce.

"A cop eventually told me I really needed to get out of there and that to be safe, I would have to leave the house until the divorce was final. So I left for four months and lost the house. After that second divorce, I completely withdrew from people. I didn't even realize I was in pain. I was just shut down.

"I guess my biggest question now to God in all of this is, 'What am I doing wrong that these things keep happening to me? And why did I not see the red flags?'

"I got entangled in a controlling relationship again right after I got saved. There was this girl at church who was very wounded and very prophetic, and she used her gift to manipulate me. I got so wrapped up in helping her that I was basically a puppet. I bought food for her and did all these things for her. I even gave her over $10,000.

"She was the first girl I opened up to after I got saved and came out of hiding. It took me two years to warm up to her and actually become friends. At first, I would talk for two minutes and then withdraw. At that point, I still wasn't interested in connecting with humans ever again. I didn't have friends at all, but she was the one that kept insisting and trying to connect. I finally allowed her in, and even invited her to my house, which was huge because my house was my sanctuary. It was a big thing for me to go on a spiritual quest with people, and even bigger to allow her into my heart.

"She had seven kids and all of them were autistic. The younger ones were affected by it the most. Because she had just gotten miraculously healed of her own Asperger's and autism, she didn't know how to live as an adult. She would come to me and ask about the basics—how to eat, how to use utensils, getting a phone, or balancing your checkbook. I allowed her to be dependent on me because she was a baby in a 38-year-old body, and my compassionate side wanted to help. I had no boundaries. If she would call me at 2:00 a.m. I would get up and go help her. I was in awe of her ability to hear God speak, so she could use that on me.

"It's funny: I could not stand kids before meeting her. I had had two abortions, and ever since the second abortion I was terrified by kids. If I saw one coming, I would run the other way. But her kids would love me and love me and love me. As soon as I would get to the house they would come running to hug me, play with me, and tell me they loved me. The genuine love that came from them was very new to me. I had never experienced somebody loving me without an agenda before. You could count on your two hands the number of times I said 'I love you' to my two husbands. I just did it because I was supposed to—I didn't know what it really meant.

"In 2012 I heard an actual, audible voice for the first time—at work!—and God told me to go to this ministry school in California. I said, 'Yeah, right.' That place seemed so spiritual and I wasn't. I couldn't imagine how I could ever fit in. But I did go, still talking to my friend by phone every day. It was when I started doing inner healing sessions that it slowly became obvious how much that was a controlling relationship. When I began talking to her about setting healthy relational boundaries, 'click!' She hung up on me. Then she started talking bad about me to people I was in class with. People would come to me and say, 'I heard you did such and such.' And I would reply, 'Do you really think I would do that?' Then later they would find out the truth and come and apologize.

"My dogs—I call them 'the boys'—were a big part of my life during that journey. I have had them for so long and they have brought constant love and acceptance to me. I have lots of short-term friends but haven't had long-term ones. But the boys have always been there. My dogs represent my place in the world."

Cami, darling,

We are going to have so much fun when you meet me up here and get to see the movie of your life that's produced in heaven! So much of what I have done to heal you is unusual and custom-made for your journey—you are truly one-of-a-kind. The angels keep coming back to watch the process, just so they can ooh and aah at seeing me operate in new and amazing ways and see your heart transform into my image. I get a lot of satisfaction out of working together with you!

I am very proud of how Jesus wove autism and Asperger's syndrome into your healing process. You pretty much had a social disorder like that yourself—you had completely withdrawn from people and vowed not to open your heart to them again. So when my Son proposed using friends with social disorders to heal your autism of the heart—perfect! What an elegant solution, and what a hoot! I just loved watching those little children—children that Satan believed he had marred and damaged—love you so effortlessly and unconditionally. What power there is in love! We laughed in pure joy. The elegance of heaven is that redemption takes everything the enemy attempts to destroy and grows flowers from it instead.

You must understand—connections like this that seem tenuous and obscure to you are seen by every eye and heard by every ear in the spirit realm. The song of redemption, of which your life is a part, is written on the sky and sounded from every loudspeaker in heaven. So when my Son reached out his wounded hand to heal you, and employed children carrying the wound of autism to love you unconditionally, and used seeing their wounds to reactivate the well of compassion in you, it galvanized every inhabitant of heaven! The angels and the saints gathered in awe to see the magnificent symmetry of how I brought healing from woundedness and good from evil on so many levels at once. And every denizen of hell understood that their terrible end had been brought one day closer.

On earth you know in part, but in heaven my purpose is clearly seen. Your life is shot through with my purpose to do good to you. No evil and no mistake or failure on your part can thwart it.

Daughter, do not take away as your lesson that the relationship with your friend failed and something must have gone wrong. It did not fail! It broke open the locked doorway to your heart—a tremendous redemptive work! Instead, look with awe at how I can take the raw material of broken, unhealthy, hurting, manipulative people and still flawlessly execute amazing plans with them.

Your friend will be rewarded with great credit in heaven for what she did for you. You will be admired and celebrated for what you did for her. And all the hurt and manipulation will be wiped away, as if it never happened. You two are great friends up here, sharing freely in the glory you helped build in each other's lives. Be comforted! My purposes never fail, and heaven truly makes all things well.

And think of your "boys"—another of my Son's creative miracles. When your wounded heart could not receive from people, I used dogs to fill your deep desires for comfort, belonging and companionship. You love your boys for what they are, because all of my creation deserves to be loved. But you also love them because through them I touched your heart. They are my gift to you, and will continue to be my gift. But now, as you perceive how Jesus has come to you through them, turn your heart toward him and he will give you all your desire to the full. Desire fulfilled doesn't lessen love, but increases it. You are going to have plenty of love for both me and the boys.

Cami, you have done so, so well in your journey to me! You have run halfway into my arms already. And I will never stop running to you and never stop making your heart come alive. It is my joy, my pleasure and my crown to do it. I love you so!

With delight,

Your Father in Heaven

The OUTCOME

"I had no clue back in the days when I was shut down that I was socially autistic," Cami states seriously. "When I read the story, though, it made complete sense to me. I was present physically with people, but emotionally I was often totally withdrawn. The creativity of Jesus to use autistic kids to love me—that blew me away completely! I would never have thought of doing that in a million years! I am in awe of how he chose to break through to my heart.

"Another thing that impacted me deeply was the idea that he used children, the very ones I had been afraid of. Back then it was a big turning point for me to go from being resistant to kids to allowing myself to experience them.

"The story took the concept of God taking what was bad (what the enemy tried to mar and destroy, like in those kids) and turning it to good—that became much more real to me. God really, really is still using his *all* of his creation to accomplish his purposes. Even after the enemy tried to steal it away, the Lord still perfectly employs it all in his plan—even the dogs! That was one of the biggest perspective shifts I got from the story.

"When I read about 'the boys,' that touched me deeply. All along I thought it was me taking care of them, but it was actually God using them to get to my heart! It was me who needed the boys, not the boys who needed me. Seeing how the Lord provided for my heart through them in such an unexpected way reinforces for me that the matters of the heart are actually far more important than anything else. Over the last few years I went from, 'I just care about tasks,' to 'I am looking at the people in the process and paying more attention to them than what is accomplished.' I always, always used to say, 'I am not a people person.' But now my whole desire is to see people walk in wholeness, more than anything else."

Contact Cami at Cami@HeavensPerspective.com.

Heaven's PERSPECTIVE

From a human perspective, Cami's life story is one of surviving mistakes, failures and great loss. When we look with human eyes, we tend to focus on what happened to her and how she felt about it. Heaven's perspective, by contrast, is about how *God* felt about what happened to Cami, and what he did to bring life to her places of brokenness. It shines a light on how he has been working behind the scenes to bring life out of death and make what was broken whole. Heaven's perspective shows off God's love as relentlessly hopeful, irresistibly good and masterfully strategic.

Seeing like heaven sees first of all requires soaking ourselves in that view of God. We must believe he is for us, he redeems all things for our good, and he is constantly growing us up into him. The belief system we hold is one of the three main components of heaven's perspective:

1. **Focus**: What is the main thing in this story?
2. **Beliefs**: What is the belief system you see life through?
3. **Connection**: Who writes your story and what is your relationship with him?

What's THE FOCUS?

Let's look first at focus. Pain has a way of getting your attention. When you suffer deeply, it is hard to focus on anything else. The human perspective (the perspective of earth) naturally locks its focus onto yourself and your pain. It experiences adversity and says, "This hurts! Get me out of this!" For instance, Cami dealt with her pain by shutting down her heart. It was easier for her to remove any possibility of love from her life than to keep her heart open and face the possibility of more pain. When your eyes are fixed on how bad things are, it is hard to see anything of the larger work of God in your situation.

The perspective of heaven moves the focus off of you and your immediate pain, and onto the activity of God in the situation. First and foremost, it's a shift from what life is doing to you to what God is doing in you. The focus shifts from the external adversity to God's positive internal work in your heart. For instance, in Cami's story the external adversity (that her friend was manipulating and controlling her) is not the focus; it is how God is bringing her heart back to life through that relationship.

Heaven's perspective is caught up in what God is building in your heart right now for others—in how he is leveraging your circumstances to make you into the person you need to be to fulfill your destiny. Instead of concentrating on what you are losing, your focus is captured by the glorious adventure of how God is shaping you for a significant, fulfilling future, and a life that changes the world. The God-story sees your life as part of a much larger story—the tapestry of human lives he is painstakingly weaving together as the bride of Christ.

Finally, heaven's perspective takes your eyes off the immediate, earthly part of your story and fixes them on its eternal happy ending. What will be the outcome of this story in heaven? How will God's goodness triumph on the last page? How is heaven working to make all things well for you forever? Cami's story focuses on how her friendship with the woman who abused her will be restored in heaven, instead of dwelling on how it is broken on earth. This fundamental shift of perspective—from the crappy situation you are in now to the God who redeems all things into unspeakable glory for eternity—lets you see yourself as powerful, free, loved, and provided for, *even if your circumstances on earth don't change.*

Belief SYSTEMS

The second component of the perspective of heaven has to do with your belief system—the lens you see the world through. Beliefs are our explanation for why things happen, and we humans have a deep need for explanations, especially when we are suffering. In our story interviews, we always pose this question: "If you could ask God one question about all this and know you'd get an answer, what would you ask?" Usually the question is some variation of, "Why?" For instance, "God, why did this have to happen? Why didn't you stop it when you could have?" Or as Cami put it, "Why did I not see the red flags?"

This leads us to another "why" question: "Why is it so important to us to know why?" The reason is that knowing gives us a sense of control, and control gives our hearts the safety and security we desire. If we know why it happened, we can protect ourselves from it happening to us again.

It's instructive that the original sin of humankind came from Eve's desire to "be like God, knowing good and evil" (Gen. 3:5). The tree that brought death was the tree of *knowing*. When Adam and Eve ate from it they were choosing to stake their future on something they could know and control, instead of trusting in the goodness of God.

Whenever we fix our desire[1] on an object or outcome in this world, like Adam and Eve did, it becomes an idol—a substitute for God. For example, if you seek marriage because you believe it will give you the love and belonging your heart craves, you've made marriage into an idol and twisted your desire. The rule of twisted desire is that these idols always turn around and bite us:

Deep DESIRES

Desires are the core motivations that drive us—the psychological needs our hearts long for. Our true desires are designed to be filled within relationship with God. He fills us by giving us himself. The *Desire Wheel* below shows the sixteen core desires.

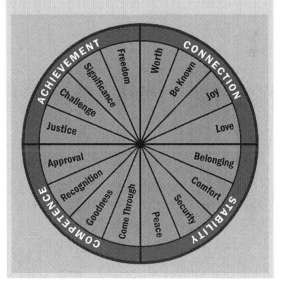

Your twisted desire always works to keep you from getting what you really want.

For instance, Cami had a deep desire for acceptance from others. When she was hurt in that area, the good desire for acceptance

---

1   *For an in-depth treatment of desire, beliefs and the inner workings of the heart, see my book* The Invitation: Transforming the Heart through Desire Fulfilled.

got twisted into a negative fear of rejection. To protect herself from what she feared, she closed her heart to people—but in doing so she closed her heart to the very acceptance she longed to receive.

The desire to know "why" when we are in pain is a twisted desire for security and protection. We try to keep our hearts safe by knowing (which we control) instead of by trusting God (whom we don't control). God rarely answers these pleas to know "why," because he isn't into giving us cheap substitutes for himself that end up destroying us rather than filling our desire.

Humanity has spent centuries wrestling with the question of why we suffer, *and yet we've never thought to ask why we keep asking a question God doesn't answer.* God appears to Job out of the whirlwind after listening to 30 chapters of the cry of Job's heart, but he never addresses why all this happened to Job. Instead, God spends the whole time talking about who he is and what he does, and never addresses the elephant in the room. What was the strategy behind how God engaged Job's heart?

The answer is right in front of our faces. Knowing why is an idol, a cheap substitute for the only thing that can actually fill our hearts: trusting a Good Father. God is not going to give us the cheap substitute. It's or our own good—he is not going to give us the thing that will turn around and bite us. The answer to the question of suffering is not to know why and thereby feel in control, but to trust God and let go of knowing why. Those who go through suffering well always come out knowing and trusting him more, but rarely having arrived at a satisfying answer to the question, "Why?"

This choice to trust instead of know leads to one of the central themes of heaven's perspective:

> *It doesn't matter what caused your circumstances, because no matter where they came from, God is going to leverage them for your good.*

I don't need to know why it occurred. I only need to know that God is for me, and that he will take anything that happens in my life and make something beautiful out of it. It doesn't matter if this adversity is my own fault, or the result of living in a fallen world, or anything else. God is for me, he will work to redeem it, and nothing can separate me from the love of God. To tell the God-story requires believing that he is good, and that his goodness is at work in every story, bringing life out of death and beauty from pain. Seeing from heaven's perspective means living out of a belief system based on trusting the goodness of God and his redemptive activity in the world.

These principles are captured in a tool we call The Three Beliefs (see graphic). The Three Beliefs are: *God is for me, redeeming circumstances to form me, and his plan is a process.* That's also a statement about who

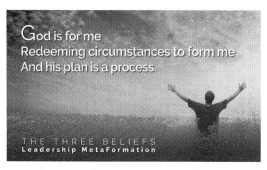

God is. First, he is a Good Father who longs to love me well. Second, his Son is the Great Redeemer, who leverages everything that happens in my life to form me into his image (that's Rom. 8:28-29). Finally, he is the God of Becoming, who is preparing me to marry the Prince of Heaven. To him, my life is not a test of obedience but a process of growing up into the same stature as Jesus in all his fullness (Eph. 4:13).

Heart CONNECTION

The third piece of heaven's perspective is about our *connection* to the Storywriter. We can have beliefs about who God is and how he operates without having much of a relationship with him (just as Cami did early in life with her picture of God as the punisher). To take on heaven's perspective, you have to actually get to know him personally. You have to feel his emotion as he engages your heart, get familiar with the sound of his voice, capture his playful sense of humor, and hang around watching him at work in people's lives. You have to get down on your hands and knees and examine the little flowers he's made, and shout about how majestic he is from a mountaintop. You will not see others through his eyes unless you *experience* his heart. This is not a matter of rational study, good theology or scholarship, but living experience. You are not, after all, relating to a set of principles, but to a person. And he is a person who is head-over-heels in love with you.

I love Scripture. However, you can't tell the God-story just by applying scriptural principles to your life. The *logos* is God's message to all of humanity, but your life story is God's message spoken as a *rhema* to you. *Rhema* is personal and experiential in a way Scripture (*logos*) can't be. That's just another way of saying you have a personal relationship with God where he speaks to your unique thoughts and struggles, and yours alone. Heaven's perspective assumes that God is still speaking and sharing the unique, secret, intensely personal things that lovers do. The God-story will always be in line with Scripture and the character of Father as revealed in Scripture. But because the God-story reveals him through *your* experiences, as opposed to those of people who lived thousands of years ago, there will always be something fresh and revelatory in it.

The faith I grew up with 50 years ago was pretty cerebral. As a boy I counted the ceiling tiles as I listened to the sermon and mumbled my way through the hymns with everyone else. I tried to follow the rules and do the right things, but there wasn't a very high expectation that my connection with God would be anything like falling in love. One of the beautiful things that has happened in Western Christianity in the last few generations is that faith has gone beyond being a purely rational enterprise. Worship became engaging, emotional and fun. We discovered our destinies, our spiritual gifts, and that we needed healing for the wounds we collected earlier in life. It used to be that emotion was something Christians were scared of. Now the emotional, intimate side of life has become a much more normal part of the Christian experience.

While we've become much more comfortable with our human emotions, we still have a lot of growing to do in connecting with Jesus' human side—especially his feelings. Just admitting that our Savior felt grief, exhilaration, sadness, loneliness, and even frustration ("You unbelieving and perverted generation, how long shall I be with you? How long shall I put up with you?") feels like a stretch. To pray, "Jesus, I feel inadequate right now. But how do you feel about me?" wouldn't even occur to us. And to ask, "Jesus, what did I do today that made you laugh?"— well, that's going a little too far. Our Jesus doesn't laugh or joke around with us, and he certainly isn't playful. He's God, after all. And gods are… well, stern, sober, serious. Distant.

It's hard to see through Jesus' eyes from this kind of overly-reverential distance, where you are comfortable with his divinity but not his humanity. We get so caught up in doing things right and changing the world for our God Jesus that we forget to compliment our brother Jesus on the sunrise, or ask our friend Jesus if he ever laid on the grass as a kid and saw animals in the clouds, or tell our spouse Jesus about our day and ask him about his[2]. We are good at serving God but we aren't good at relating to him. Connecting with his excitement, his grief, his passion, and his playfulness in everyday situations is what teaches us how to bring heaven's perspective to earth. The God Jesus became the human Jesus to bring heaven to earth. Connecting with his human side helps us do the same.

God STORIES

Bringing heaven to earth is the focus of the stories that follow. They are organized into chapters around a reframing tool we've

developed called the *Seven Frames* (see graphic). "Reframing" is the word life coaches use for inviting a person to look at things from a different perspective. So the *Seven Frames* are seven specific viewpoints we use to see a story as heaven sees. Each one is given as a contrast between the human viewpoint and the heavenly viewpoint. For instance, while Cami saw her broken friendship with the gal who manipulated her as a failure, God saw it as a success, because it opened her heart to relationship.

2   *If you are intrigued by this idea of relating to Jesus' emotions, try my book,* Questions for Jesus, *or the free* Questions for Jesus *mobile app that goes with it (available in the Apple app store and the Google play store).*

Where Cami evaluated by her performance, Father evaluated according to relationship. That's the *Performance vs. Relationship* reframe.

Each chapter begins with an overview of one of the *Seven Frames,* which is then illustrated with two God-stories. (Chapters seven and eight add bonus stories about the *Heaven vs. Earth* frame.) The stories are told in three parts, like the account of Cami's life you just read. The first section is the individual telling the "before" version of their painful experience, as we heard it in our original interviews. Next, you'll read the God-story: the same events, but seen from heaven's perspective. The final "Outcome" section relates the impact heaven's perspective had on that person.

We didn't pick out only the most dramatic narratives to put in this book. These stories are typical of the tales we hear when we ask ordinary people to share one of their most painful experiences in life.

One of our story subjects (Sophia from Chapter 10) wondered if there was a way that people who identified with her story could contact her. A number of other storytellers felt the same way, so their stories include an e-mail address at the end. If you are inspired by a story, feel a kinship with that person, or want to connect with someone who understands your similar situation, feel free and drop them a line.

Now let's begin our journey with the first frame: *Performance vs. Relationship.*

Chapter 2:
PERFORMANCE VS. RELATIONSHIP

*"...I write to you, children, because you know the Father.
I write to you, fathers, because you know him who is from
the beginning. I write to you, young men, because you are
strong, and the word of God abides in you, and you have
overcome the evil one."*

(I Jn. 2:13-14 RSV)

The verse above has always intrigued me. It appears to portray the different perspectives we have during different seasons of the Christian life. There is a fascinating symmetry to it, as the descriptions of both children and spiritual fathers and mothers are quite similar. But what do John's phrases mean? I think I had to get old to really grasp it.

When you are a new believer, there is a beautiful simplicity to the Christian life. You've just met this God who loves you, and all you want to do is be with him and build relationship with him. He is God and you are not, and you are learning to live in obedience and trust with the God you are getting to know.

As you grow up in the faith, you enter a new stage. This season focuses on the mission: what you are *doing* for Jesus. You discover you are strong, you learn the principles of walking in faith and you launch out with vision and energy to make a difference in the world—to overcome the evil one. Life gets more complicated as you learn to balance the competing demands of God, family, self, work, and calling.

When you graduate from that stage to become a mother or father in the faith,

there is a surprising return to a simpler, more childlike faith. All the models, principles and practices you learned in the previous stage don't disappear, but they recede into the background as one thing becomes paramount: knowing him. You go back to your relationship roots with God. But this time around is much richer, because all the wealth of knowing him from the beginning is behind each encounter you have with your Savior.

This lifelong rhythm—moving between seasons of relationship and being to seasons of productive doing—is also true in the smaller cadences of life. Life regularly swings between seasons that focus primarily on outward mission and ones that major in inward renovation[1]. Strangely, we call the inward seasons of intimacy (where outward performance is removed from our lives to make room for knowing him who is from the beginning)

---

1   For an in-depth treatment of the seasons you'll pass through on the journey to your destiny (and a cool tool for creating a timeline of your life), see The Calling Journey *by Tony Stoltzfus.*

"deserts" or "valleys," and we struggle to escape them and return to what we think of as normal, productive life. This "kicking against the goads"[2] happens because Western culture tells us our value and worth is based on what we produce. Our identity gets wrapped up in what we do, so when our work is taken from us, we feel worthless and unmoored. God's challenges this false identity, rooted in our performance, to help us let go and return to finding our worth in our relationship with him.

In our humanness, we naturally tend to focus on our performance and what we are doing for God. But Father's main agenda is something totally different: deepening our relationship with him. *He is much more interested in being with us than using us.*

That's what the Performance vs. Relationship reframe is all about. When doing and accomplishment fail to give our hearts what they long for, God moves to pull us back to him—often by taking away the role or dream we've put our identity in! We lean in to his purpose in these seasons when we stop fighting to get our doing back, let go of putting our performance identity and just enjoy the time to be with him.

The stories that follow demonstrate how God works in us to shift our focus from performance to relationship. As you follow along with Allan and Noah in their journeys, watch how God leverages their struggles to draw their hearts into deeper intimacy with him.

---

2   *Goads were sharp sticks you prodded an animal with to get it to move. If you visualize an animal kicking its hind legs backward into the stick when it is prodded, you'll get the idea. Resisting only makes it hurt worse!*

An Audience OF ONE

At 61, Allan Jefferson is still writing "God's songs for broken, hurting people who need restoration." As a part-time substitute teacher in the Manchester schools, he is able to convey his life message to kids: it is OK to fail; it's only a bump in the road that points you in the right direction. "This whole season has been planting that message in me," Allan muses tearfully. "Maybe it started when I was a kid, when everything was so perfor-mance-oriented I thought about suicide. That's carried through my whole life. I have written many of my songs out of times of despair and lingering depression."

As a pastor and worship leader for many years, he feels called to create emotionally-vulnerable worship music that leads people into intimacy with God. But Allan still struggles with deep questions about who he is and what he is supposed to be doing in life.

"I haven't only been a musician, and that has created confusion about what I am supposed to be doing. Am I a pastor or a musician? I am 60 years old and I feel like I have missed the boat. I haven't accurately discerned my life's purpose until now. I don't see a lot of fruit from my 25 years of pastoral ministry. I don't feel like I have succeeded as a pastor, and I spent so much time pastoring that I haven't succeeded as a musician.

"I have always known I was called to sing. When I was 30 I felt called to travel and minister in song. I was building a recording studio but I sold it so I could afford to go to the U.S. to pursue that dream. An evangelist invited me to start a church with him there and be his music minister. After two years I felt unsettled in spirit, so we moved to Nashville to find work in the recording industry. But the doors never really opened for me—I was shattered by that. An opportunity came my way to have an income there working as an English teacher. But the idea in my mind was that I was called to be a musician for God, not a teacher. Looking back, it was the provision of God, because I needed a job. But I didn't see it.

"Then we starved for three months. God never came through for the traveling ministry I thought I was supposed to do, because he had already come through for me with the teaching job. But because I was so idealistic— it wasn't the music career I wanted!—I turned the English job down. So then we had no money, no job and no opportunities. It was a difficult time. I felt like a foreigner in a strange land. I don't feel like I responded appropriately to the call of God on my life at that point.

"To make ends meet, I started a music school where I taught piano, voice, composition, and more, and I did substitute teaching during the day. I went out at 6:00 a.m. and got home at 9:00 p.m. I never saw my kids except on weekends. It was just too hard. One morning I sat up in bed and exclaimed, 'We should go back to England and start a church!' Our pastor agreed and ordained us, so we went.

"We still have 50 people after 20 years. Most of the people are happy with our church, but growth is very slow. We love our people, but I don't feel pastoring is a good fit for me.

"Around the time we first left for the U.S. I received a prophecy that I needed to function in the pastoral role to give me an understanding of people and learn to develop the heart of a shepherd. Then after we had been pastoring the church for several years I got a prophecy that God was calling me back to music—that I had a gift that was lying dormant and I needed to give myself to it. That took me by surprise. My dreams for music had all fallen apart years before, and I hadn't touched music for ten years. My identity had become that of a pastor.

"So it was very difficult to make the shift, because I'm an all or nothing guy. It was very hard to die to being the leader and give up my baby. The Lord was saying I should give my wife the administration of the church so I could give myself more to music. So from that point on she has shouldered running the church, although I still preach.

"But I was still divided. I was saying, 'God if I am called to be a musician, why am I still pastoring?' We had two sources of income—my wife's part-time salary at the church and my music business. We'd lived off next to nothing for 25 years, but at that point my music business was really growing, and the hope was that we could eventually live on that. But then my sales dropped by over 80% and I had to go back to teaching full-time.

"At one point I just quit preaching—I felt like I had had enough. If I wasn't any more successful as a pastor and preacher than this, why keep at it? I finally told God, 'I will write your songs, record your songs and sing your songs, but find yourself another preacher.'

"Then I had a meeting with Joseph Prince. His assistant pastor told me, 'You need to preach more'—only a week after I told God I was going to quit! It was God affirming that I really was in the right place.

"Pastoring has developed my relational skills, given stability to family, and taught me compassion for people. But I feel like I have wasted my life trying to help people without much success. My wife says we have sowed into hundreds of people, but what sticks with me is the people who have left. I don't see much fruit.

"What am I proud of? I'm proud of my kids: they are a good heritage. I'm proud that we are still in ministry, and still married. I am proud of my songs. I've done eight albums, and I know they touch hearts for God.

"But my main concern is for the stewardship of what God has given me. If I had been more focused on music I would have had more impact. I pray the Jabez prayer, that God would bless me and increase my sphere of influence. Still, I am virtually unknown, and I don't feel like my influence has been very significant. But I want my life to count. I want to go to heaven and hear him say, 'Well done!'"

My Allan,

Son, thank you for your love and your service!

You remind me so much of one of my other special favorites: Job. He got his knickers in a twist because the world didn't turn out like he expected, and so he assumed that something had to be wrong with the universe. Job got angry with me and thought I was the problem—you just get angry at yourself. Son, no one is upset with you but you.

Don't you seek me with all your heart? Don't you want me more than anything? Of course you do! Your sweet sacrifice is visible to all of heaven, where the angels hold you in high regard. They stand in awe, and kneel to worship me over the wonder that your heart has become. There is no argument in heaven about whether you are approved. No one here would even think of questioning whether you belong. You are a hero of heaven.

Understand that the core of my will is not that you do a certain thing, but that we do it together. I care much less about whether you were at a certain geographical place at a certain time than I do about our relationship. Your call is not a place but a shared journey. My will is that you are in me, and you are right now in the center of my will.

You say, "My life has accomplished little, and I have had little influence in the world." Don't you know that you have influenced heaven itself? Do you realize that your human life, formed out of mere atoms of dust, is held up before all the principalities and powers in the heavenly places as evidence of my power to restore? Do you know that your name is known in hell, and that hell fears you? Or that your songs are in constant rotation in my courts? All of heaven and hell know you: is it really so important to be known on earth? Everything you do and feel is constantly in my thoughts. Do I need to argue with you to convince you how valuable your friendship is to me? Must we go to war over my desire to honor you for who you have become?

Son, remember: what you have done to the least of these you have done personally to me. You have not "wasted your life helping other people." You have been a doorkeeper in my house your whole life! You are a true son to me. Your first and primary call is just to be my mate. If your song touches my heart, you have changed the heart of God, and the impact of that change ripples through heaven and earth. That is the greatest influence on the universe there is or ever will be. So be content; your life is of great significance to me.

I am deeply honored by how you have sacrificed some of your own dreams for your family, and brought them into my friendship as well. It is a great act of love when you do so much to bring those you love most into my family. Because I do not commonly reveal what might have been, you do not realize how pursuing your own dreams earlier in life would have ended. It would have destroyed your family, estranged your children and destroyed you. You would have felt like you never saw them, and they would have felt like they grew up without a father. I never wanted that and neither did you. Together, we have walked a better path.

So take comfort! You have faithfully preserved what is most important in your life! Heaven does not look on your life and see defeat. We see glory and success.

Allan, the great strategy of the enemy in your life has been to make you flounder in the muck of despair. The seed of your childhood despair remains in a deep place of your heart, and it has been a doorway that allows the enemy to trample your heart and skew your thinking away from the view of heaven and toward discouragement and failure.

I do not hold that against you. How could I? You were a child when your heart was wounded. It is not even your own voice that speaks out of that pain—it is the voice of the enemy. But you are not who that voice says you are. Have you noticed that when you are ready to give up on your role or think you have failed, that my voice is the one that affirms your value and calls you back? I have never agreed that you are a failure, and I never will.

Your life-long journey of healing and restoration has brought you to the point where we can now close the door on that despair for good. Your whole life and every experience in it was necessary to bring you to this point. There are no shortcuts, and you have missed nothing.

Now, join me in completing my good work, the crowning achievement of your life. Will you let go of judging your life and measuring your success, thinking it will give you significance, and simply fall into the ocean of my pleasure with you? You do not need to protect your heart from disapproval: you are approved! You will not be abandoned: I will never leave you. You cannot fail, because you have already succeeded beyond your wildest dreams with me.

You are enough. You, Allan Jefferson, man of God, are enough for me. Embrace that, believe and rest in it. You are a true son and I say well done, good and faithful servant! Enter into the joy of your master.

So pleased,

Your Father in Heaven

P.S. The angels are psyched about trampling all over that ugly despairing spirit that's been after you. They are truly beautiful and terrible when they get their war on!

The OUTCOME

"This last week," Allan begins, "Has been a major, final resolution of a life-long question: 'Who am I?' I've handed the church over to my wife, and she is fulfilled in her role as a pastor and teacher. For the first time the other day I corrected someone who introduced me as their pastor, saying, 'No, I'm not the pastor—my wife is! I'm married to the pastor!'

"At the *Living from the Heart* workshop, where I received that brown leather journal with this story in it—that was a life-changing moment for me. Soon after, God spoke to me in an inner healing session and asked, 'Is it enough to be a son?' I discovered that I am not a doing machine. I am a human being God Himself wanted a relationship with. For the first time, I resolved the performing thing. The guilt and sense of failure are gone, and it's so good to get that devil off my back.

"The end game is, 'While I was down here on earth, did I learn to love?' The real fulfillment is in your relationship with God; because if that isn't enough, then you are just striving and pushing and hurting people. If your motivation is performance, he can't give you your destiny or it will destroy you. It has to be a natural outgrowth of walking with him instead of trying to please him. That shift has been the most significant thing God has done for me in 60 years.

"Now, I can give myself room to fail. I love myself because God loves me. I don't have to succeed, and I can extend grace to myself, which means I can extend grace to others. Just to give you a picture of what my past was like, my kids would hear me coming up the stairs and a sense of panic would grip them as they thought, 'Here comes dad—what haven't I done?' Now, when I ask someone in church to do a task, my focus is not on how they perform, but on the opportunity for relationship in it. It's about whether they feel loved, not if they succeeded at the task. My whole orientation has changed. God loves me and what he wants is to be with me. He wants relationship, to walk with me in the things I do.

"God has been speaking to me from the verse, 'He has shown you, O man, what is good; and what does the Lord require of you, but to do justice, and to love mercy....'[3] He wants me to learn to love mercy. Not just doing it because I have to, but *loving* it. He said, 'I want you to see every moment as an opportunity to show mercy—to look for those opportunities where people fail, and *love* giving them grace in the middle of it.'

"I still have a long way to go! It's not something that comes naturally to me, but it's a beautiful way to live. Learning to love mercy is one of the biggest transformations that has ever happened to me.

"Years ago, I was a striving, performance-oriented perfectionist—it was never enough. Today I am happy. I am happy to be a husband. I am happy my children love their new father. I am happy with a small church, and if no one listens to my songs I am happy with an audience of One. It is, indeed, enough to be a son! But now that I am happy, and God is happy, I think he has plans... ☺

"To sum it all up, it is worth the struggle to know that God loves you. It's difficult, but in the end, God redeems everything you go through. He catches your tears in his bottle and lets you know it's going to be okay. And his grace is big enough to do that in spite of your mistakes. In fact, he loves you so much that his perfect plan is made of your mistakes. He works his plan even through all your perceived failures."

Contact Allan at Allan@HeavensPerspective.com

---

3   *Micah 6:8 RSV*

You Are ENOUGH

Noah Troyer chose Jesus as Lord at eighteen, after "deciding whether to get drunk with friends and throw my Bible into the ditch or start believing what's in it." Now 67, he has pastored both full time and bi-vocationally for over 20 years, seeking to "equip the church for her finest hour." The financial struggle of being a small-church pastor and Noah's deep desire for relationship have both been at the center of his story.

"From early in life I learned to believe that providing for my family all depended on me," Noah begins. "When I was five our family moved out of a Beachy Amish community to southern Lancaster county, and started a little church with a few other people. But we were always on the fringes and isolated. We had a dairy farm where we milked morning and evening, so between that and school there wasn't time for a social life. I was a loner. When I was 18 my dad had a heart attack, so my brothers and I started running the farm. I got so discouraged trying to make ends meet—I was only making about $50 a month.

"I remember standing out in the lane looking at the stars one night, weighed down with all the isolation and the loneliness. I wanted to form friendships, but I didn't know how. I did not know how to relate to women, either, so there weren't any in my life. I said to myself, 'This is the way it is always going to be. I will always be isolated and without friends.' I didn't realize that I was beginning to close my heart off to protect myself.

"During college things started to change for the better. I became part of a traveling gospel team that helped open my heart again to relationships, and I developed five very good friendships with men. Next I went to seminary, where I lived with a lawyer and worked for him to scrape up enough for room and board. I was standing out on the golf course next to his house one night and God told me, 'You belong to God. Wherever you go you will always belong to me.' Even though I was by myself in a new town, he was beginning to address my sense of isolation and alienation.

"During my last year in seminary I got a 'Dear John' letter from my girlfriend in Pennsylvania and I said, 'Here we go again, Lord.' But he replied, 'Your desire for companionship is a gift from me.' I felt like he was asking me to surrender that desire, so after a few days of struggle I let it go. Shortly after that I met my wife, in the summer of 1977 when I was 29. The beauty of her face captured the beauty of all the women I had been attracted to in the past. We were married a little over a year later.

"After being an associate pastor for six years, we started a church plant when I was 39. That was a valley season! We had a strong beginning with 80 people, but a year later two-thirds of them left, saying it was a mistake to even start it. The leaders came to my house and said I had a spirit of control, and I should either repent or leave. That was extremely painful. They finally pulled out and started another group down the street, and the same control issues came up in them again!

"Before the church plant we had taken a week of training with Victorious Ministry through Christ (an inner healing ministry), and received a lot of healing for past hurts. We learned there that we were valuable to God, and we felt very valued by those leaders. Year after year we went back for more. So when we were attacked in the church plant we had a base of acceptance that carried us through. The project failed, but I was not a failure.

"We certainly learned a whole lot about leadership in that church plant. After the blowup, I asked three pastors from the denomination to examine me to see if I was operating out of a spirit of control. I was a little afraid that they would find that I was a bit controlling and lose respect for me, but they actually affirmed that I was challenging the congregation to grow, not being controlling. That experience taught me to be more honest about my own strengths and weaknesses, and not to think of myself as being worthless. I learned that God would bring us into an abundance of relationships even in the midst of the hardship.

"Since two-thirds of the people left, I had to go get a carpentry job, and that's where my financial anxieties took root again. I didn't always have work, so I would go to Chicago for a week at a time and build decks. I was never sure there would be enough, and that made my wife anxious, too. I'd wonder, 'Will it always be this way?'

"That period of bi-vocational ministry lasted about a decade.

We had to work pretty hard to make ends meet. I remember once helping build a barn for about five dollars an hour. I was fearful about the future, and had a significant inability to trust God for finances. During that time both we got involved with Amway through some friends in Chicago. I justified it as making money for family, but it wasn't good for my family connection. It seemed like whenever I had a break I was making Amway calls. That business never prospered.

"When I was 50, we finally closed the church plant down and I went into full-time carpentry. I got very discouraged, and felt like a failure with God, wondering if I had been put on the shelf or if I would ever get back to being in ministry. I didn't know how to pray my desires, so instead of being filled I just felt defeated. Every morning at the jobsite, I'd step out of the truck and say, 'Lord, I am doing this unto you today.' Through those painful events and significant growing pains, I learned some valuable lessons. But the inability to trust has cropped up again this last year in a whole different area.

"I took my current pastorate in 2008. After seven years, I'm having to confront my inability to trust God in the areas where I have leadership responsibility. The big question is the leadership structure. When I came here, I realized it had developed without a lot of forethought. We have both elders and a council, so there are two competing structures I am supposed to be accountable to.

"Things came to the surface when we discovered that the divorcees in the congregation were thinking of themselves as second class citizens. At first, the elders were divided over whether a divorced person could lead. But after much study, prayer and discussion, we came out with a very good conclusion and were all in unity. But when we took it to the congregation the administrators on the council blew up. One said, 'I have been here twelve years and we still don't have a clear decision making process!' I had to talk one key congregant out of leaving over it.

"So the last year has been a struggle, and it still hasn't been resolved in a healthy way. There is hope, but some on the council don't see eye to eye, and relational disconnects are hard on me. There have been times I have been unable to sleep after council meetings. I wonder, 'Are we coming to the end of our time here? Will I end up somewhere else?' The congregation is fragile— there are only 50 people—and we need a fresh start.

"And rethinking the structure pushes my buttons, too. Will the administrators ever be on board with the vision? Will I be controlled by others? Will we have a structure I can't live with? I am afraid of losing the freedom to be myself, and afraid of losing the respect of the congregation. It is all challenging my inability to trust.

"So this has been a huge growing and stretching time. I am sleeping better, and I am trusting Jesus more. But I still question whether I have attached my heart to my picture of a dynamic church instead of to Jesus."

Noah,

You are my man. Your past belongs to me, just as you belonged to me in your past. You belong to me in the now. And wherever you go in the future, you belong to me. Your belonging is assured—you never have to wonder or worry about this permanent fact: you are mine.

Brother, in the same way you belong to me, I approve of you. You are enough for me. You have done enough and become enough to satisfy me forever. Who you are gives me great pleasure—it is a joy simply to think of you. You never need to worry or wonder about something that is set in stone in heaven: that I approve of you.

And you are free in me. Sometimes, I lead you in paths you don't know just for the adventure of it all, and to feel you nestle up to my side. Sometimes I put an open field in front of you just to see what you will choose, because I delight in watching you exercise your freedom. And sometimes I simply walk beside you, enjoying the freedom you carry. Nothing can shake this eternal reality—you are free in me.

I have something I'm very excited to show you today! It's a picture of your life—from heaven's perspective. It's a story about the longing of your heart that I've known since before you were born. Your tale is this: that I will take your whole life to give you the approval, belonging, connection, and love your heart yearns for.

I saw you on the farm lane at night as a young man, as hope was dying in you. In that low moment you said to yourself, "This is the way it is always going to be." I was not offended by that statement (although it broke my heart). I do not even look at it as a wrong choice. You embraced that belief because it protected your wounded heart— numbed it, so your isolation and awkwardness wouldn't hurt so much. I understand. But it is a dangerous thing to turn off part of your heart.

Now, here is what your statement sounded like to heaven. What I heard was the cry of your heart, a prayer for deliverance, and a great challenge. "Really?" I thought to myself. "Does Satan think he has won you so easily—that this is all I would give to a true son of mine? Does he think my arm is so short I can't save Noah?" That kind of thing makes me mad. And when I get angry, justice springs into action. In response to the cry of your heart, I set heaven in motion to accomplish one thing: to spend the rest of your life giving you the connection and love your heart wanted. That is your story, and your message: that I am family to the broken and loveless and lonely. Here is what I did.

First, I brought your wife into your life, and established your life-long connection with her. That was an important step in prying your heart back open and giving you hope. Then, I arranged for you to get healing in one of the few places it was available at that time. You did not just choose to go to Victorious Ministry through Christ—no, you were sent. I personally arranged for you to be in a place that spoke value into you, and showed you who you were and what you were worth.

In that experience, you learned your worth in times of success and good fellowship. Next, I wanted to teach you your worth even when things failed and went bad, so that you would not be vulnerable or easily thrown off by hard times. So I placed you in a church plant.

Do you know that most of that whole situation was for you and your benefit? Do you know that with all the people who were involved, and all the hopes and dreams there, that the center of the story was my heart to connect with you? That is how much you mean to me: I will move the lives of many people to get your heart. (They were also processed in that season, but that is another story.)

What was most important to me in that season was not whether the church succeeded or failed, but that you were hoping again, and opening your heart to the future. That was very good, and I was proud of how far you had come.

Of course, when the thing fell apart, there was always the chance that you would close up your heart again, and maybe even never come out. But I knew you, and I believed in you, that you would meet me there instead of running away and hiding—and you did! I was so proud—especially when you allowed yourself to be evaluated by other pastors. That was another important step. You feared losing respect and relationship, but instead you received vindication.

You're welcome! It was my pleasure to give it. I don't often allow my leaders to see this, but you were allowed to watch the dysfunction of those who accused you play out in plain view. I wanted you to know that I was not angry with you, and that you were approved by me even when the work you attempted to do fell apart. And you got it: the work failed, but you were not a failure. Well done!

From heaven's perspective, the period after you left that church, when you had to get a job and felt like you were really struggling to trust me financially, is not called "The Days of Mistrust," but "Living from an Open Heart." The first time you experienced that kind of pain in your life, you shut your heart down and stopped hoping. This time, you stayed engaged and felt it the whole way through. It did not worry me that you struggled with your feelings, when I was so excited to see you stand up and hold open your heart even when it hurt. That was well done! Every time I talked with Father about you, he commented on your courage and your progress. We were both so pleased!

Just so you understand our perspective, we expected you to struggle with trust. We don't expect a human life to be transformed in a day. It takes a process. And your process was going forward very well. So when you look back on that season, don't see it as defined by mistrust or fear, but by courage, victory and growth. That's how we see it—and we see truly.

And what of today, when you feel you struggle with trust about your church's structure and government? I do not see mistrust. What I see is a heart that once dealt with pain by closing in on itself, standing with courage and hope, meeting me and being transformed. There is no greater joy for us in heaven than to see Father's children full and free. It is a tremendous pleasure to cheer them on as they achieve the victory of a lifetime, as you have, birthed through a lifetime of his good work in them.

Noah, when heaven looks at your life, it sees nothing but Father's good hand, guiding, redeeming and loving. We see you enjoying the desire of your heart—one that you almost gave up on as a young man—and we think that is awesome.

So come up with us, and see your story the same way! You belong here in heaven. You have heaven's approval, always. And you are free in me—free to enjoy me forever! Truly, nothing can separate you from the love of Father God!

Your brother always,

Jesus

The OUTCOME

"This story gave me a pretty different perspective on my life!" Noah exclaims. "For instance, what I thought of as distrust and struggling with finances Jesus saw as keeping my heart open to growth. To think that my journey was actually about learning to live with an open heart... I'd never seen it that way before. Even when on the surface everything seems to be falling apart, I am in God's process of learning to trust. God is actually forming me.

"I realized that God has taken a lifetime to convince me that he is filling my longing for love, belonging, approval, and freedom—that he is working to fulfill those desires in me. Knowing that he really approves of me as a person brings a settled awareness of the presence of the Father, Son and Spirit every day. All I have to do each morning is open my heart, and I receive security, approval and love in him, in his person.

"Since I got the story, I've come to know Jesus as my approver. He approves me before the Father. Life is about Jesus' relationship with me, not about my performance. I grew up in a church where it was all about performance, but now it is about the relationship that he has with me.

"This week I've been asking Jesus questions about the story of Peter walking on water[4], where Peter was in the boat and asked Jesus, 'If it is you, command me to come to you on the water.' Jesus is constantly wanting to come closer to me, and wanting me to come closer to him. His presence has become very real in my everyday life. As I open my heart in the struggle I am in today and ask him to bid me come to him on the water, I experience his companionship and being with me. It brings a settled calm. To think I can just take five minutes to sit and ask him a question and experience that! Every day he is investing in me.

"There is still a struggle with fear and mistrust at the church. Right now we're pretty fragile. If one family leaves it would throw our whole financial picture up in the air. So there is a practical, everyday application to all this. But I am more at peace with it and at peace with being here. Stepping out of the boat for me right now is about taking relational risks to have authentic

---

4   *A meditation from the book,* Questions for Jesus *on Matthew 14:28.*

relationships with people. This is a huge growing time for me in forming real relationships. I've realized that Jesus' ability to trust the Father is actually living inside me, in my spirit. Having access to that, I am able to trust more, which helps me be calm in the middle of conflict. And that makes me more effective.

"His presence is increasingly real to me, and the invitation to partner with him is growing. That really energizes me! By immersing myself in the Word, resting and not being anxious about stuff, the Holy Spirit helps me live out who I really am in him."

Contact Noah at Noah@HeavensPerspective.com

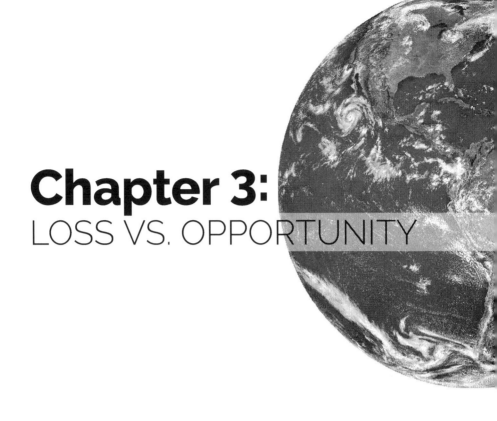

Chapter 3:
LOSS VS. OPPORTUNITY

"Indeed, I count everything as loss because of the surpass-
ing worth of knowing Christ Jesus my Lord. For his sake
I have suffered the loss of all things, and count them as
refuse, in order that I may gain Christ..."

(Phil. 3:8 RSV)

Years ago on a coaching call I remember listening patiently to a young man on the mission field tell me his tale of woes. He had married the local bishop's daughter, but the bishop wouldn't give him any ministry opportunities. His church at home wasn't supporting him like they promised, he was struggling to feel at home in a new culture, the church he was trying to plant still only had 11 people, and his friends had abandoned him. It certainly didn't sound like a fun situation.

"So let me try to sum up," I offered as his narrative wound down. "You still want to be in ministry—you just don't want to get hurt anymore. Is that about right?"

"Yeah, pretty much," he replied.

"Then how will you ever really know Jesus?" I inquired. "His life was defined by suffering. If you never suffer, you'll never be able to connect with that part of him."

There is a deep, intimate communion with Jesus available to those who've experienced deep pain that Paul calls "the fellowship of his sufferings" (Phil. 3:10). Fellowship happens like this. When we first meet a new person, we ask them about where they are from, their hobbies or what they do at work because we are looking for points of connection. If we both love the Atlanta Braves, for example, we've found a common interest, and now we can fellowship around that shared experience. We have something to talk about.

If you've suffered in this life, you and Jesus have a defining experience in common you can talk about—you have the fellowship of sufferings. If I am feeling betrayed by a friend, I might ask, "Jesus, how did you deal with being sold out by a kiss? That had to hurt!" Or if I am just weary from entering into others' pain to bring healing to them, I could ask him, "Jesus, is this what it felt like when the woman touched your robe and power went out from you? After it leaves, how did you recover and get it back?" Or even, "Jesus, life kinda sucks right now. When did you feel like that?" Your common suffering lets you connect with each other in ways that someone without that experience simply can't.

We have a high priest who has been tempted in every way that we are—who understands the human experience from our point of view. One of God's purposes in having his Son share our experience is making that fellowship possible. No matter what pain we are in, it always contains that opportunity to connect deeply with him.

Loss VS. OPPORTUNITY

In every loss, there is an opportunity. That's the Loss versus Opportunity reframe. One of the best ways to use it is to refocus from whatever temporal thing you've lost to the opportunity to fellowship with Jesus you've gained.

Here's an example. A friend just lost a job he was deeply

committed to for ten years in an office power struggle. It was a crushing blow. But instead of sitting at home licking his wounds, he discovered an opportunity. Today he is out sailing the Pacific Ocean in the beautiful boat he and his wife just bought, getting his captain's license so he can fulfill a lifelong dream of taking people on ocean adventures. He found an opportunity in the middle of his loss.

Loss often becomes an opportunity for destiny. For most of us, our calling comes out of an experience of suffering. We go through grief or loss, or identify with it in others, and dedicate our lives to alleviating that suffering. Our loss becomes an opportunity for great service.

Loss can also be an opportunity for learning and growth. Have

a group of people think of the most important things they've learned in life. Then ask, "Did you learn that in the midst of joy or suffering?" They will almost all say, "In suffering!" The loss became their opportunity to learn. Or ask them if their greatest growth happened in comfortable times or hard ones. Growth is the opportunity that comes to us in difficult seasons.

No matter what loss you experience in life, Father can make something beautiful out of it—that's Romans 8:28. You just have to find the opportunity!

As you read the following stories, look for how God took relational losses in Angie and Angelica's lives and transformed them into opportunities for growth, learning and destiny.

Let Us FELLOWSHIP TOGETHER

> *"…the kindness of God leads you to repentance"* (Rom. 2:4).

At 61, Angie is a highly-relational, ENFP personality type[1] whose calling is to create spaces where people can grow and develop into God's plan for their lives, because "that's what I missed out on." Passionate about retreat and camp ministry, her joy is to share the Jesus who is a best friend who will never leave you.

"I grew up in a Christian home, and was baptized in fourth grade into my parents' and grandparents' church which was the Disciples of Christ. As the youngest of four, I have three brothers who are a lot older than me. I mostly had a wonderful childhood. However, at ages two and three my parents went away on vacations for a month at a time. That sort of gave me an abandonment thing.

"In college I seemed to have one foot in the church and one in the world. I'd always had a heart for church but didn't understand obedience, and I didn't know the Bible. When I was seventeen at church camp I felt called to be in full time ministry. But what could a woman do in ministry back then? There weren't many roles available for women.

"I took a whole new step in my faith when I went to an Emmaus retreat when I was 44. That weekend I experienced the love of Jesus unconditionally, and saw that his way was the only way. My marriage was in bad shape at the time, and my husband was not following God in any big way. I quit trying to do things I didn't feel right about to make the marriage work, and chose God's way for me.

"When I was only seventeen my father passed away—he was the nicest guy ever. He had a heart attack, which was very sudden and unexpected. That night was my first date and he didn't want me to go, and when I drove back home through the pasture there was an ambulance in the yard. I ran into the house, and there was my mom and a fireman, who told me my dad had died. While I was fighting the tears, he said, 'You need to be strong for your mother.' So in shock I clammed up and sort

---

1   *The ENFP in Myers-Briggs personality type is an extroverted, a big-picture thinker who naturally sees the potential in people and tends to have open-ended plans and expectations.*

of stuffed it. I disassociated and didn't let myself feel anything. I was a senior in high school, graduation was coming up, and I distracted myself with that.

"Right after my father died I started dating a guy who became my high school sweetheart. He was president of the youth group. I didn't really like him as much but he really liked me.

"At 21 I graduated with a psych degree because I thought that would be good if I went into ministry someday. My mom had just remarried and home wasn't the same, and I wasn't really sure wasn't sure what to do with my life at that point. My boyfriend and I had broken up and dated other people during college, but now we were both back home. I thought that maybe I should marry him because I didn't know what else to do. I wasn't really in love, but he was a Christian and filled the bill. So I did.

"We were married ten years and we had two little girls. Three weeks after the wedding I thought, 'If we send all the presents back, can we somehow not be married?' But you couldn't do that. He was an introvert, a very black-and-white, analytical engineer. I remember thinking that I wasn't getting my needs met, so would I join things to fill the void. He could never understand that. I went to counseling for my marriage, and to develop personally, just trying to get help.

"My counselor challenged me to talk to my husband about needing more from our relationship. I tried to give him a wake-up call, but he was focused on getting his degree and passing the exam and just didn't understand.

"He finally told me he had to move to California for work, and snapped, 'I'd rather live in a hole than live here with you.' He said I was a big burden to him, and he didn't want to take care of me. So he decided to move out when I was still thinking we could make it work. 'This doesn't have to happen!' I remember thinking. 'You aren't supposed to get divorced.' But another part of me was relieved.

"I moved back home to Florida at 32 and we got a divorce. I was so sad for my kids, and wished I would have been able to make it work. I wanted to do the right thing and care well for my kids, and I couldn't. That's my biggest unanswered question: 'Why?' It isn't supposed to be this way. It's contrary to all my concepts of God and life, and I never thought it would happen to us.

"Since I am all about relationships, it was hard to be divorced and single again. I remember being in church and all my relatives and friends were there, but I was feeling so far from God, thinking, 'I am here but I have nothing to do with this at all.' Church was my relational tribe and my support, so I got involved anyway. Praying and reading the Bible aren't things I remember practicing, but I did go to church. I knew I wasn't doing things right, and felt so far from relationship with God. I was dating, because I just couldn't be without someone. I was desperate. If God was not in the picture... well, I just needed that affirmation.

"At a class, I met my second husband. He said, 'I'll go to church with you.' At the time, I was involved in the church in all these ways, but had no personal relationship with God. It began again after I remarried.

"We were married for sixteen years and had one daughter. He would go out of the country once a month because he said he needed to think! I started to feel like something was rotten in Denmark. When I found out what he was really up to I confronted him about it, but he said, 'I'm not willing to change anything I'm doing.' I didn't know what to do, so I went to my pastor and told him about it. He said, 'He's fifty years old, he's not going to change.' What my husband had done made the decision to let go and leave him easy. I was relieved in a way, but I probably detached myself from it again so I wouldn't feel the hurt.

"I'm in my third marriage now—I feel really bad that I messed up two times. For a while I thought that if I knew then what I know now, I could have made things work. But I don't believe that anymore. I've let go of it. When I talked that way to my daughter (because she didn't grow up with her dad), she would say, 'Mom, let it go. There's no way you could have lived with him.' Maybe I will never know what could have made it work.

"I feel like I should have known better. I wish that I had had the confidence to be on my own instead of having to get married. I wish I had been taught obedience, or been given the space to develop into who I was. I feel kind of condemned. It's embarrassing to tell people this is my third marriage."

My Love, My Heart, My Angie,

First, before anything else, I want to tell you how grateful I am for you. I am thankful that you have allowed me to make myself at home in you. I am so thankful I have had a chance to know you, and know you well, when there were times in your life where it looked like we might be estranged. I am grateful for your gentle heart, for your fierce love of people, for your awe and wonder at the world. I am happy that you've had the courage to try again with relationships, even after you failed and felt the pain of it more than once.

Remember the good, Angie, like I do. Heaven has this quality: the pain and the mistakes and the embarrassing things pass away (there is no embarrassment in heaven!), and only the good remains. And many things that were thought bad on earth are so transformed by what Father does with them that they become good in heaven. Whatever is exposed to the light becomes light, as Scripture says. This describes how Father takes what was meant for evil and produces good out of it, and even brings it into heaven. Much of what you call "failure" is already present to us in heaven in redeemed form, and we see and marvel at the good Father has brought from it.

So don't go around ashamed of a "failure" Father has already converted into glory! Don't wait to forgive yourself when Father's forgiveness has already transformed your mistakes into part of the majestic tapestry of his work on earth. No! Enter into forgiveness, enter into grace, and see your mistakes morph into powerful weapons in your hands to overcome evil and bring good into the world. This is the destiny you have long been prepared for. Let go of your shame, take up the courage and confidence Father has placed in you, and revel in them!

This longing in you, that many times has come out in pursuit of romantic relationships, is actually a desire for me. I put it in you. What you yearn for is to sit with me and share the deepest joys, pains and intimacies of life, every day for the rest of your life. The love you seek is here, for free, in me. And it is my will that you have it! All you have been through in life has served to bring that hunger to the surface and direct it toward me. You have felt for and found me, just as I willed, and I am not disappointed in one step of your journey. Now here I am, just what you have always wanted! And this is your season to drink deeply of me, and find all your desire in finding me.

I, Jesus, have a special gift for you. You and I both know the pain of failed relationships. I knew that Judas would fall many days before he actually did. I saw the twisted desire take over his heart, and as John observed, I was troubled in spirit. Do you know that I asked myself some of the same questions you do, like, "What could I have done to make this relationship work?" I, too, had to hear Father say, "It doesn't matter." Since we have both passed through this same fire, let us fellowship about it, and share our mutual sorrows and our joys. My gift to you is the intimacy of those who have suffered together.

You and I both know the pain of longing for a love that isn't returned. Oh, daughter, how many days did I see your heart in pain on your couch at home, wishing and wanting that a different man would return to you from his work! And every day you were disappointed. Come, and let us fellowship together. I felt the same pain with the rich young ruler, who couldn't bring himself to love me more than his money. And I feel the loss of every heart that chooses hell when it could have heaven. So it is like sweet incense to me to share my heart with someone like you, who understands from experience what my experience is like.

You and I also know the suffering of watching ones we love grow up without a father. Come, and share that with me. We know what it is like to sit in a house of worship in our hometown and feel completely disconnected from the lives of the people we once knew. It was the folks in my hometown who had the hardest time accepting me for who I was (they were the first ones to try to kill me, long before even the Pharisees). Come, let us fellowship together about it. And we both know the frustration of wishing someone had taught us. My best shot at that ended when my parents ordered me home from the temple when I was still a boy. Come, let us fellowship around this desire, and I will teach you everything you want to know, and we will both be satisfied.

The very act of this fellowship, of creating intimacy from our shared suffering, will serve to redeem your painful times and bring them into Father's Kingdom.

This is your destiny: that every failure and loss in your life will be redeemed into a point of deep intimacy with me. The powers in the heavens will see and know the immensity of my power to rewrite history, and the glory of my redemption, through the story you once labeled a failure!

I am not ashamed to call you my sister. I am proud to be your brother, and proud of the story we have made together—a story that ignites worship in heaven and instills fear in hell. You are mine! And I want all of heaven to see and know it!

Bursting with pride,

Your Brother Jesus

The OUTCOME

"When I first read the story, I was just crying and crying," Angie recounts. "To realize that the longing that came out in my pursuit of romantic relationships was really a longing for him, and that he wanted to have a romantic relationship with me touched me deeply. It was a real 'ah-ha' moment. And the very first paragraph, where he said he loves my gentle heart and my love for people—that felt like he was speaking just to me. I felt so affirmed.

"The part of the story about failed relationships—that he has failed relationships, too, and we have that in common—that has really stuck with me. He knows what it is like for kids to grow up without a father, and we share that. That was a revelation.

"I am in a bit of a wilderness season now, and so I just talk to him about it. 'Jesus, how did it feel to be so cold or so hot out in the desert, or to be hungry?' And we share that suffering together. My suffering is being redeemed to bring me closer to him.

"He feels so much more real and present to me now. Like yesterday when it was pouring rain outside, and I just sat and visited with him. To be content to just sit there with him and talk about our relationship—it made me smile. I used to worry my prayers. They were all about what needed to be done. But now— Jesus approves of me! He loves hanging out with me! So we don't have to talk about business. We can just be together. If I can do that every day, I can do *anything*. All the other stuff will all work out.

"The story gave me a deep feeling of approval from Jesus. That was just like, wow! It came home to me that Jesus died on the cross for *my* sins, for everything that I've done, and it doesn't matter anymore. In the past, I could say that for other people, but it didn't seem like it applied to me. The fact that he saved me and has taken away all my mistakes sunk in in a whole new way. He has taken my divorces away, and I am approved.

"Having that sense of approval helps me to feel accepted. When we came to the heaven room at the workshop[2] where they were separating the sheep and the goats in front of the door of heaven, I thought to myself, 'Oh no! I might be a goat!' But now

2   *Angie received her story at the* Living from the Heart *workshop.*

that Jesus has taken away my divorces, I can see the good in my life, that I have done good things. I'm not afraid I am a goat anymore. I belong.

"To see what I had done in such a better light gives me the courage to try again. It has helped me concentrate on my marriage now. The part of the story where it says, 'I have been searching for him all this time'—well, I knew in my head that he was all I needed, but I still got married again to fill the void in my heart. But now I am really understanding that he is everything, and my relationship with him is what makes all the other relationships work. I am being drawn closer and closer to him. Now I know the importance of obedience. I focus on him and his instructions are right there in front of me, and he is teaching me what to do every day.

"I think part of the way I have gotten into bad relationships in the past is by being a pushover, and this has made me more confident to stand on my own. And that is better for everyone in the long run."

Contact Angie at Angie@HeavensPerspective.com

I Can USE ANYTHING

Angelica moved from Indonesia to the U.S. when she was eighteen. Raised a Catholic, she always knew about God, but feels she really made him Lord and began to know him intimately only six years ago. At the end of her rope, she cried out, "I know you but I don't feel you. I really need to feel you! I never hear you talking like people do in the Bible." That began an adventure where God led her to quit her job and go to an underground church in China. "I didn't understand what they were saying, but it touched my heart. God came alive to me there." Now she works to "build people through coaching so that the way they see God is transformed."

"My spectacular failure story," Angelica recounts, "is being 36 and not married. I grew up in Asia, where the expectation for girls is that you go to school, get married and have kids. My parents think I am a failure. I feel it myself sometimes. They think that I am 'expired'—that I have passed my expiration date to get married and have kids. My mom says I am too old and beyond too old to get married. Nobody will want to buy something past the expiration date. I've felt lots of pressure about that. Probably my biggest question is: 'God, what have you been doing? Am I any closer than I was before in getting ready for marriage?'

"In my 20's I had two longer-term relationships. The first one happened before I was a believer, during a time in my life where I had a lot of fear in me. It only lasted for a year. The expectation I was living out of was, you meet people, you date and then you get married. I was just going with the flow. I don't think I even knew at the time that I was looking for love—I can name that now.

"In the second relationship (which lasted three years) we got engaged, but he broke it off when I was 29. We originally met at work. He was French, and we were so different! I was just looking to get married, so after dating for two-and-a-half years I began to pressure him. 'What are we going to do? Where is this relationship going?' I told him we should either get married or end it. He wanted to go back to France, and I didn't want a long distance relationship. I wanted to get married, but I didn't want to go to France. I didn't speak French, and I didn't trust him enough to be there for me. I was scared, and a lot of my fear and uncertainty about who I was and what I wanted was coming out. I think that scared him, too.

"I was brought up as a pretty rational person, so I started in that relationship with my head, but then slowly moved toward my heart. That was the part I didn't know how to manage. He was surprised by the depth of the heart-level stuff that I shared at the end. I wanted assurance for my fears, particularly that he would be there for me if we went off to France. I think some of our mutual attraction was because we each seemed like we had it all together, but my insides were pretty messy and that shocked him. I wasn't even sure what I wanted from him. I didn't know how to express it. I just felt the fear.

"He was confused by it all. I was growing in my capacity for emotional intimacy, but he wasn't. As I began to share more of my feelings, he wasn't able to dig deeper and go to the same places. So even as I was growing in starting to feel things, we were growing apart.

"I had my education, my work, my friends, my apartment, that relationship—I was meeting everyone's expectations. I had been away from my family in the States for ten years without feeling lonely. But that moment when he ended it… that was the moment I really felt alone. The enemy was talking in my head too, saying, 'See, nobody loves you. Your parents don't love you (our relationship was pretty bad at the time), he doesn't love you and you are all alone.' I left that relationship feeling so hopeless and empty. It was the darkest period of my life.

"At the time, I wouldn't have known how to say this, but if he had not grown with me I would not have been able to connect with him. That would not be the marriage I truly want. But still, having it end felt like another relational failure. And I was not pure in that relationship. I feel dirty, and that adds to the feeling of failure, that I am no good.

"Emotional intimacy wasn't something I learned in my family. I've never seen my dad cry. We rarely sat down at the dining table to talk, and even if we did, there was no such thing as a question like, 'How was your day?' or, 'How are you feeling?' or even, 'Do you like this?' We never really talked at a heart level.

"I never heard my parents say, 'I love you' to each other, and never saw them holding hands. They do practical stuff together but they don't seem to connect at the emotional level, and I have a hard time feeling connected with them, especially with my dad. For instance, there was a ten-year period when I wasn't home and they never took the initiative to call me. I started out calling them every week, but over the years the intervals got longer and longer. I got really angry about how it didn't feel like our relationship was mutual. But when I confronted them about it they just gave a practical reason that it was easier for me to call them. They were living in the practical and didn't see how it affected me emotionally.

"I wouldn't want their marriage. They want me to get married for practical reasons, but I would not like that. Heart connection has become pretty important to me. I have friends, but it doesn't mean I connect with all of them at the heart level. I want to be able to talk heart to heart.

"That's been an important insight: that my deep desire is for connection. I have seen myself as a relational failure because of the pressure that's put on me. This conversation is showing me I am not a failure.

"Right now I'm in a season where another guy is pursuing me. He is a really nice guy, but I wasn't crazy about him at first, so I am stumbling around trying to reconcile the whole thing. I want to get married, but I am struggling with that he doesn't seem to fit the total picture I have in mind. But God has been changing how I see things in relationships."

Dear Angelica,

I want to thank you for not getting married yet, and saving yourself for me. You may feel like you have given away something you shouldn't have in relationships with men, but to me, you've safeguarded for me the most intimate, important, precious thing: your heart. What a gift! Heaven celebrates its giving!

Being married to me has its benefits. It is not a marriage of convenience, but one of constantly growing depth and intimacy. It is not a marriage where I ask you to leave your country and come to me, but where I leave my country in heaven and come to you. Because I left everything behind for you, you can (and you do!) trust me to always, always be there for you, no matter what fears or desires come out of your heart. The more you know me, the more you love and trust me. And the more you love and trust me, the greater your capacity to love and trust others, and to attract those who know how to love and trust.

Oh, daughter, you would have been so disappointed to be married before now! To pledge your life to a relationship that couldn't give you what you most wanted, that in fact would have left you rejected and withdrawn and deeply hurt—I would save you from that. It was me who raised the questions in your mind, me who made you uncomfortable with where things were. Yes, your concerns got accreted with fear and pressure from your parents, but know that the original movement in your heart was my protection.

I also want you to know that I incorporated that three-year relationship into my plan for opening your heart. You grew during it, you risked more of your heart as it went on and you began to open up to him. When the time was ripe and it ended, you were in touch enough with your own heart to reach out to me in a way you never could have before. Our relationship owes a debt to that relationship—it was a midwife for our intimacy. I look at it and am satisfied because my purpose was accomplished. So when you think of that relationship, don't see it as a failure, or even as impure—see that my redemption is so powerful and all-encompassing that I can use **anything** to open hearts and bring people to me. See that and celebrate what I did through it!

Zaccheus came to me because his greed destroyed so many of his relationships that he yearned for a connection he couldn't make on his own.

Mary came to me because her life as a prostitute left such an aching wound in her heart that she was willing to risk everything to find real love. Paul—and heaven laughed at this—came to me because his religious offense was so great he could no longer live with himself. For all of them, their pain brought them to me. So you are in good company! Don't despise the grace that brings life out of brokenness. I died so I could give that gift, and it is the greatest joy in my life to give it.

My dear sister, I want you to understand your parents' hearts, and have compassion on them. At the root of it, their wish for you to be married is a desire for you to be happy. They want you to succeed in life. They have wrapped that desire in a picture of what they believe will give it to you (marriage), which limits me. And they put pressure on you to be happy because of their brokenness—because they look bad in their culture and feel bad about themselves as parents if you aren't married. You can always tell when evil is at work because it is so twisted. It takes their good desire to see you happy, and twists it into a pressure that actually makes you unhappy.

I am going to do something about that for you. I want to move their hearts out of their brokenness so they can love well. Here's how you can come alongside that transformation: fill their desire. They long for you to be happy. So tell them about your happiness and how blessed your relationship with me is. They long for you to be successful, so tell them of your successes. They are afraid of failing as parents, so tell them how they have succeeded. They are afraid of looking bad, so tell them how good they look to you. I am working to turn their hearts toward you in a fresh way. It is another part of my long-term plan to prepare you for intimate, connected relationships. Let's have fun working at it together!

Your husband in heaven,

Jesus

The OUTCOME

"The story now feels deeper than when I first read it," Angelica muses. "I am on the other side looking back (I got married!), and it touches me more now that I can clearly see Father's heart for me. At first I said to myself, 'Okay, I will have to trust that this is true.' But now that I have gone through the whole process to the end, it is more tangible that God really is good to me.

"The first time through the story made me cry, because it touched me where my heart wants to believe God is for me. My head was saying otherwise, so this big argument was going on inside me—'How can he be good? How can this all be good? I still have the pressure from my parents and I still am not married—how can that be a good thing?'

"Getting to the other side of those fears was a long process. In my journal I was asking God a lot of questions, like this one: 'How can this be good, because I am still alone?' I filled up an entire journal on that same kind of question, over and over.

"He replied with different things at different times. For instance, I went to a friend's wedding and as I was sitting at a table in the corner and watching, I felt anxious. I tried to socialize but I really wasn't happy and wasn't being very nice to people. Later when I was journaling I asked God, 'What's going on? Why was I feeling that way?'

"He showed me that when I was little I *liked* to go to weddings with my parents. My dad is a pretty respected man, with lots of friends, and at weddings his friends would come up to him and say, 'Oh, this is your daughter? She looks so pretty!' That was the *only* time that my dad expressed being proud of me in front of other people. I got approval from him there, but never anywhere else. A light bulb went off in me and I realized, 'I was looking for my parents' approval! That's why I felt anxious and wasn't very nice to the people at the wedding. Nobody gave me the approval I was waiting for.'

"Dillon (my husband now) and I worked together, so I knew him and knew that he was a good person. I pretty much saw him every day. He asked me out with him, but after a couple of dates I decided he didn't fit my list of things I wanted in a husband.

And the fear came up in me that it would be awkward to be dating someone from work. So I said, 'No.'

"But God kept nudging me. He was not saying that this was the guy for me, but that there was nothing wrong with exploring the relationship. So I would say to Dillon, 'Yes, let's give it a try.' And then I would think in my head, 'No, this isn't going to work,' and break it off again.

"It took a while to work through all my questions. For one, I didn't really trust God. I wanted what was on my list, and he was trying to give me a bigger picture. But the more I walked through it, especially in the couple times I said 'No,' I would see a different side of Dillon. Even though I broke his heart, he was *still* really nice to me. And that was what God was trying to show me about himself. I saw who Dillon really was when I wasn't with him, and through that I saw who God was even when I wasn't with him. That's what I needed. I needed to know in my heart that God was for me no matter what.

"There was a turning point where I finally grasped how much God loved me and I began to develop compassion for my parents, because I understood that they really did love me, too. I finally got it in my heart and not just in my head. I guess it just became so real in my heart how much God loved me, so much so that I realized that whoever he puts with me it must be safe and good. I don't have to figure it all out, get all my questions answered and protect myself, because he will. And that enabled me to say, 'Yes' to Dillon.

"I knew in my head that God loved me, but now I know the depths of how my heart needs his love and how dry and empty my heart was. And now he just fills it with more and more. The more I am hungry and open my heart to his love, the more he pours in—to overflowing."

Contact Angelica at Angelica@HeavensPerspective.com

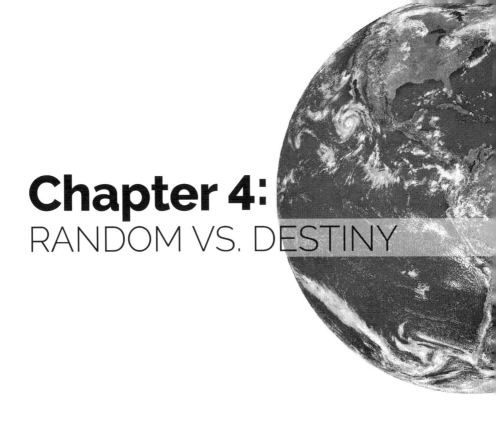

Chapter 4:
RANDOM VS. DESTINY

"All is well, and all manner of things shall be well, and you shall see it."

Juliana of Norwich

Years ago, as we were mingling before our young married small group meeting, I asked a gal whose husband was on a six-month naval deployment how she was doing. Brittany began to share a bit of her loneliness and the feeling of being an outsider. Single friendships she once had had changed since she had gotten married, and it was awkward to try to hang out with her married friends all by herself. She just didn't feel like she fit.

Trying to help her get some perspective, I started inquiring about her calling. We hit pay dirt when Brittany explained who she was called to reach in life. She had always felt drawn to people on the fringes, those who just didn't fit into any group. They were the ones who stand by themselves at school, who aren't popular enough to hang with the cool kids but don't fit in with the stoners, either—that's who she wanted to reach.

I was chuckling inside because the connection between Brittany's circumstances and her calling suddenly became so obvious. One of my destiny principles is, "You get to live the life of the people you are called to reach." That's what God was doing with Brittany. She had been seeing her husband's deployment as a random, lonely experience, but now I was able to reframe it as preparation for her destiny.

When we suffer, we are drawn to those who've suffered similar things. We instinctively know they will understand us, that they will say something genuinely helpful instead of offering up empty platitudes. For instance, if your baby was stillborn, the best person to comfort you in that pain is someone who went through the same grief and met God there. That shared experience is the qualification, the credential that opens the door to your hurting heart. God provided Jesus with this credential, too: "For we do not have a high priest who cannot sympathize with our weaknesses, but One who has been tempted in all things as we are, yet without sin" (Heb. 4:15). And, "For since he himself was tempted in that which he has suffered, he is able to come to the aid of those who are tempted" (Heb. 2:18).

By experiencing being alone and not fitting into the social groups around her, God was giving Brittany the credential she needed to touch the hearts she was called to reach.

Random VS. DESTINY

That's the Random versus Destiny reframe. Many things in

our lives that seem meaningless are actually God at work, preparing us for our destiny in ways that are not always obvious at the time. Moses fled from the palace into the desert with his crushed dreams, where he worked like the slaves he once owned for 40 years herding sheep. Were those wasted years? Moses probably thought so at the time. And yet, when he led the people out of Egypt, what he learned in the desert became crucial for his destiny. Among a group of people who'd spent their entire lives in the lush Nile delta, Moses was the only one who knew where the water holes were and where the trails went. He was the only one in Israel who understood the language and customs of the local tribesmen, or could identify which plants the cattle could safely eat. Only Moses had ever climbed a mountain, or camped at an oasis, or knew how much food and water to carry to traverse the desert. Without his 40 years in the wilderness, he would have led the whole nation of Israel to their deaths.

I can identify with Moses because my experience was a lot like his. Now I coach ministry leaders, but my preparation years were spent as a furniture designer, drawing, selling and speccing custom woodwork. How I longed to get into my ministry calling, so I could do what I was born to do! For fifteen years I asked God if I could leave, and every time he said, 'No.' Life was passing me by, my peers were doing exploits for God around the globe and I was stuck in a little town in Indiana designing expensive furniture for rich people who didn't need it.

A funny thing happened, though. When I did finally enter ministry, what I learned designing furniture became the cornerstone of my success. Coaching didn't exist 30 years ago. So God put me in an occupation where my role was to take people who had a dream (of a neoclassical desk, or a French Country armoire) but not the technical language to describe it, and to ask questions to draw out what was in their hearts. For fifteen years my job was to meet new people, believe in their dreams, and put those dreams on paper. My job was not to give them what I thought they should have, but what they already had in their hearts.

What perfect training for a coach! Coaching is not about giving people advice—telling them what *I* think they should do—but asking questions to draw out *their* ideas. God arranged for me to get paid to learn what I was born to do, and I didn't even realize it! That muscle of believing in people was so ingrained in me by fifteen years in furniture design that it made me powerful as a coach from the very start.

Destiny PREPARATION

If you committed your life to Jesus in your early years (like most Western Christians), your twenties and thirties are years of preparation. As one very wise man said to me when I was that age, "Up until you are 40 it is all about you. If you get any real ministry done, it's gravy."

A mistake the church has made in the last decade or two is telling people that no matter your age and station in life, you should be in your destiny NOW! But it doesn't work that way. In my studies, the average time it takes for a Christian to move from making Jesus Lord to fully entering their destiny is 31 years![1] If you have used your long season of preparation well, you'll accomplish more for the Kingdom in a year (maybe even in a month) in your fifties than you could in a decade in your twenties and thirties. God invests in preparation in your early years for vastly greater returns later in life.

And he is amazingly efficient and endlessly creative in how he prepares us! There is no telling what crucial skill or character trait he is slowly building in you, often without you knowing what it is for or even what he is doing.

What the Random vs. Destiny reframe does is make those connections. As you read the next two stories, look for how God transforms seemingly random or even tragic events into destiny-building experiences for Larry and Jacob. The more you study the ways of God in building people, the better you'll get at recognizing what he is up to. Then you'll stop fighting to get out of his process (like I did) and embrace it instead.

---

1   *I did in-depth interviews and timelines of over 50 leaders and informal in-terviews with many more to establish that figure. See the book,* The Calling Journey.

Flourishing IN CHAOS

"For I know the plans I have for you," declares the LORD, *"plans to prosper you and not to harm you, plans to give you hope and a future"* (Jer. 29:11 NIV).

Larry Turner has been in health care for the last 40 years, working first as an EMT in 1976 and then a nurse and a trainer of nurses. He fully gave his life to God when he was overwhelmed by Jesus' loving presence several years after losing his brother in an accident.

"I am highly relational, and my call is to bring unity and interdependence to the people around me," Larry asserts. "I call myself a 'here and now' person. I live in the moment, and whoever happens to be under the same streetlight as me is the audience for my calling. New people come into my life and I can create a safe place with them really quickly. I am also ADHD. I didn't know that until three or four years ago, but it makes a lot of sense. For instance, my school career was less than illustrious. I first cut class in kindergarten! No matter what school I went to, my parents were on a first name basis with the principal. I knew I was different, but I didn't know what it was.

"Working as an EMT and on the cancer unit at the hospital, I have been in a lot of emergency situations. That pattern started early in life: my brother died in my arms as I did CPR on him. Then I witnessed an abortion in nursing school. It took a long time to process that. I remember wishing I could have saved that baby. This belief got attached to me early on that 'you can't save anybody.' I couldn't save that baby or save my brother. God has done so much through me over the years—I've resuscitated people, I've seen healings—so how does that lie still stick around? I guess that's my biggest unanswered question in this story: 'Can I save anybody? Can I help anybody?'

"The worst mistake I ever made was on a hunting trip I took with my brother and a friend back as a freshman in college. We were driving through the night, and our plan was that one guy sleeps while the two guys in the cab stay awake. About 3:00 a.m. I was driving through the Mojave desert, and my friend and I both fell asleep at the same time—a five-second nod-off. We were towing a jeep, and when the wheels went off the pavement I jerked back awake and made a correction. But that swung the back of the truck around and we rolled over. My friend and I were bruised but alright. My brother was sleeping in the open bed of the truck, so he got the worst of it. When we found him out in the sage brush, he was still breathing but he'd been crushed by the truck. We did CPR, we tried everything we knew, but he still died there in my arms. It was bizarre. It didn't feel real.

"He was my hero, my older brother. We were living together and had just become good buddies, and this was a special trip. It was a double kick in the gut to lose him and to be responsible for his death. I was numb for a really long time—the whole family was. I never felt they blamed me, but we were like zombies walking around for the first month or two, and only gradually came back to a semblance of normal. The next six months of school were just going through the motions and surviving.

"That loss was also kind of the last straw in my parents' marriage. They divorced a year or two later. After the initial numbness wore off, I came down with a bad case of survivor's guilt. That led to several years of real darkness—drinking and weed and that kind of thing. That destructive lifestyle ruined all my relationships, including with my future wife. For me, the biggest pain is when I am hurting other people. I thought of taking my own life, but out of that desperation I turned to God at 24 and started putting my life back together again. He just kept meeting me along the way. Brenda saw the change in my life, and within about six months we got back together again, and then got married.

"But I still lived under that guilt for a long time. Finally, about ten years later, I was teaching my little son to paint the house. He had wanted to know for the whole year before where uncle David was, and while we were painting I told him how he died. A year later, when he was seven, out of the blue he says, 'Do you feel sad when you think of uncle David?' I said, 'Yes.' And he said, 'You know, if he hadn't died that day God would have taken him in some other way.'

"That was a breakthrough for me. I let go of a lot of the responsibility I had carried for the mistake I made. It is what it is. We all live the number of days we are supposed to live. I felt a weight come off me that day. When I think of David now, I think more about our love for each other than I do about the pain.

"Here's another similar experience. I was in nursing at that time, and my knees started to give out. I couldn't work and it looked like the end of my career. I was told I needed two knee replacements at 45 years old and I thought, 'Oh crap, these will only last ten or twelve years, and I'll have to do it again. This is not what I need!' I was so worried about our future. That was the day I caved in and said, 'God, if I can't walk, how can I provide for my family?' Jesus replied, 'Oh, Larry, you don't provide for your kids!' So I surrendered and said, 'I don't care what you do or how you do it, you are going to be my Lord.'

"After that encounter with God, I let go and that was a big weight off of me. A couple of weeks later at church this little old lady of 70 stood up in a meeting and said to me, 'You've helped other people and now it is time for your knees to be strengthened.' And my knees were miraculously healed!

"I'm thinking of another experience in letting go that impacted me deeply—this time it was more potent on the inside than out. I was in youth ministry for fifteen years. The church staff put me in charge of the college age group, and it was an awesome experience. The group went from ten to forty, and it seemed like it was going really well. Then the management fired me. They cleaned out the whole youth ministry and put the pastor's kids in my role. What made it so hard was that I had let leading that group become my identity. It became an identity crisis. I was Larry the Youth Minister, but it ended and I no longer was who I thought I was. Could I ever really help anybody, or would it always all fall apart?

"People who are let go from a church position usually leave the congregation, but I didn't feel like I was supposed to. That was another big wilderness experience. For six months it was like I was invisible. Nobody called me, nobody came to see me outside of church and no one asked me how I was doing. After six months of that I was heading home in a rainstorm from a church meeting and it all came to a head. I was so hopeless and lonely I had to pull over to the side of the road and get down on my hands and knees in the pouring rain. I just said, 'God if you don't show me that you are in this, I quit!' And his presence came again like when I first got saved, and he just threw his arms around me and displayed his love for me.

"It's funny because the minute after that happened, the minute I let go, I became visible again. Literally every day, someone from church called me and told me how much my ministry had meant to them.

"I began working on a cancer unit, and instead of saving lives, I took care of people at the end of life. In my first six months at that job, a guy came in who had been born on the same day I was. He had gone in for a checkup and found out the next day that he had leukemia—so advanced that treatment wouldn't help. He had weeks to live. I asked, 'God what do I say to a guy who is facing *this*?'

"I went into his room and I just spontaneously started to cry—and that was exactly what he needed. His brain wasn't processing how dire his situation was, and that helped him move quickly to closure. What God did as soon as I started weeping was we bonded. This man needed a companion to help him navigate the last two weeks of his life.

"I am not afraid of death. I am able to unite with my patients around it and help them live powerfully right to the end. I go to the hard places with them, and I've found out that their hearts would open to me if I united with them. Then all kinds of things happened that wouldn't ever happen otherwise.

"I don't think I would have been able to do that without the experiences I've had in learning how to let go. When the patient dies, it isn't a failure; it's a part of life. I had to reconcile myself to that cycle of life in my own story and discover how God is good in all of it. I take the wisdom from those experiences and plant it like seeds in my students, and they are now way better prepared for nursing than I ever was. And that's the kind of thing I have to pass on to the next generation."

Larry, my friend,

I am especially fond of you!

I want to show you how I designed your destiny. Your whole personality and gifting was made for connection and relationship. So I said, 'Aah—let's make him a vessel of unity, to bring people together.' You felt the pain of death much earlier in life than most. I did not will that, but when it happened, I said, 'Let's redeem that and make him into one who can bring unity and life to others who are facing the pain of death.' You had ADHD from when you were young. I didn't create that, but when I saw it I said, 'Perfect! It will give him the ability to move on, and stay in the moment instead of getting stuck in the pain that touches him in his calling.'

Working with those who were dying, I knew you would need to be able to let go, or the grief would crush you. So throughout your life, I have brought you to the point of deep desperation, where you deeply let go, so that letting go would come easily to you. You received a graduate education in letting go, because it was vital to your health.

I knew that hope and being able to see the good would be crucial to being able to bring life in those situations, so I crafted your personality type to be strong in those areas. Death cannot be administrated or planned or scheduled—it comes when it comes, whether we like it or not. So I protected your heart by not giving you a strong need to have schedule and order to function. What many see as a weakness has been a great strength for you: those who love schedules love to know what to expect, because it gives them a sense of safety and control. You were created to live within the unexpected moment, to comfort those whose expectations of life had been dashed. You were made just right. I look at you and say, "That is very good!"

I want to open a new realm of hope for you—the hope of understanding in greater depth what actions here mean in heaven. When you were let go from your youth pastor position, that was a painful time. You had to wrestle with what happened and how you had been treated. You had to come to the point of surrender and letting go. And once you did, it was as if you became visible. People began to come to you.

But thus far, you have only seen what happened from the perspective of my dealings with you. I was also dealing with your church. It wasn't that I held back people from coming to you and then let them come when you did what I wanted. It was a situation where a breakthrough was needed—both for you and for them. They needed to break through the fear of speaking out that kept them silent, that inability to overcome relational awkwardness and reach out. What happened was, when you got a breakthrough, they got a breakthrough through you. You tore through the curtain, and they walked through the rent behind you. Your releasing the situation to me released freedom in the spirit realm, and it freed them to get beyond their own obstacles and see you. That was not me—you did that! It was your response to me that changed them and set them free. Don't think that you can't change people: you already have!

And you have also changed heaven. Every act of love and service adds glory to heaven. There are streets filled with homes and happy spirits that would not be here without you. That is why I am so grateful to you for meeting me, for entering my service and for loving well. You have erected part of heaven that all will enjoy for eternity.

It is an eternity where your brother waits, joyfully anticipating your arrival. He wants nothing more than to throw his arms around you and shower you with heaven's love, and I totally approve. Do you know that he shares in the glory of all you have given and accomplished on earth? Wrestling with his life and death made you who you are. And who you are is beautiful. Every person you have reached out to, every life you saved, every student you taught, every cup of water or tray of hospital food you brought to a patient—all will be credited fully to his account. His is not a truncated life in heaven, but a full one, through the connection I made between the two of you. You will share life in a way you never would have otherwise, because his death so shaped your life.

Understand, too, that he has no regrets. To him, nothing has been lost, and everything is gain—even death (we laugh at death up here).

So hope in this, true son—that heaven makes all things well, beyond your wildest imaginings. All shall be well, and all manner of things shall be well, and you shall see it.

Your Father

The OUTCOME

"When I read the story, it was really good to step back and look at my life as a whole like that," Larry says with a smile. "It feels like the same message I've been hearing lately from God— 'I've had a plan from when this first started that includes all the falling down and getting up.' It's all in the plan. And it feels good to know that my mistakes and weaknesses are covered. That takes a lot pressure off. It's shaped me to where I have to forget that perspective to fall into the place of frustration and anxiety. And when I do get frustrated, I tell myself, 'You are forgetting again what your story is.'

"Speaking of funny—I got this dog recently, and whenever I get frustrated and drop an f-bomb or something like that, he runs over and gives me this look, like, 'Hey man are you alright?' Now I am apologizing to my dog for my attitude! He will drop a *bone* to look at me when I am frustrated, and he runs over to try to comfort me.

"When the story said, 'I didn't create that, but when I saw it…' I saw again the spontaneity and adventure in life that God encounters with us and enjoys. He enjoys being surprised some-how. I don't understand that but I get it. When I bought my kids presents when they were little there was such a joy in watch-ing—I didn't know how they were going to react when they opened them. It's like that with God. Life is such a joyful adven-ture that God shares and enjoys watching. I just love it that he enjoys me! I want Jesus to be happy—and he is the happiest guy I know. But to know he gets happy about *me*—that's the thing that rescues me from my frustrations. Just to remember, to be with him in the now and experience that, pulls me back.

"I notice that I get frustrated quicker than I used to when I am not with him. So there is no alternative right now other than being in his presence. And that has been the life-long longing of my heart. He is helping me moment by moment to live my life for every moment. He loves it, and I love it.

"I also want to comment on the part about my ADHD, where the story says, 'Here's what I can do with that.' It has been like that in all my jobs. I am always in unscheduled, unplanned situations. Like right now, things got so chaotic on one of the programs at the school that they asked me to come in and take over teaching it and try to help the students finish out the semester. And it went from this horrible mess to one of our best programs; there was so much healing that happened in the students. Just like it says in the story, I can go into a place that has no schedule and no map and create a map as we go. The Dean has seen that and he'll say, 'Let's send Larry in. He'll try anything!'

"I am seeing the utility of how I am made—that I am built to function in chaos where others can't. My hope is not in getting the circumstances to calm down, but that God has the circumstanced in hand. And I help others do the same. I am seeing that he has this plan that he made before the foundation of the world and we get to release that plan. When I hear that I am made to go into these painful moments and let go—I feel the power in that.

"It's just so cool! It is not on me to undo the chaos, but to just keep being willing to wade out in it, to even get over my head in it. Like one of my friends says, 'The pain is in the resistance.' Knowing this helps me not resist. I'm in Jesus' hands, we're in this together and he loves it. And it is going to work, even though I may not see how."

A General's WORTH

Jacob Gerber served for years as head of a denomination in a southern state until he was voted out in 2009. He did not leave with a sense of closure or that his time in the role was over, but rather felt like he was ousted in a coup set up by friends and those he'd invested in who'd bad-mouthed him untruthfully to colleagues.

"After I left the state director role," Jacob recalls, "I spent some time finishing up various projects. We bought a house upstate on 60 acres and started fixing it up. I did some conference speaking and also went on a five-week missions trip to Mozambique. In the fall the Tennessee district where my roots are asked me to do an interim at a larger church. The church grew a bit, and the missions budget increased a lot. It was a wonderful ministry for us for seven months.

"I brought my friend from Mozambique over and raised $300,000 for him in seven states. In the fall, I started doing 24 credits a year of grad school—that taxes my abilities! I'm also doing some fund-raising for a Bible college, being a grandfather and rehabbing a barn, too.

"But it has been hard to feel put on the shelf. To be sitting in graduate classes listening to people with half the experience I have… that was so chaotic. I had to take a preaching class—I've preached thousands of sermons—and if I ever preached as badly as that prof my wife would rebuke me. And the books we read! A lot of them just weren't helpful.

"People we knew and respected told us, 'Don't go looking for ministry, let ministry come to you.' I felt like that was good counsel. But we've waited a long time, and I wonder, 'Are we still on your map, God?' As a 'D' (dominant personality style) I can make things happen, but I felt I wasn't supposed to do that. I am leaving my father's house like Abraham did: leaving what was safe and easy and what worked for something unknown.

"But my biggest question right now is about the relationships I had. I wonder, 'God, are you talking to these people? What is happening in their lives that I don't understand, that the ones I walked so closely with won't reach out and get in touch with me?'

"I don't think I was ready for how many people I had invested so much in… I haven't heard one word from them. For me, if someone comes to my mind I usually just call them. I see that as God talking to me, prompting me to reach out to them. I have done that for many years as a pastor and leader. So it seems like if God was talking to others in reference to me, that I would get an e-mail or a call—or *something*.

"Whatever my wife and I were in our roles in the district, we embodied that we never cry alone. That was my ideal. Now here we are. So there is the individual pain of those relationships disappearing, plus the pain of saying, 'What I thought we were as an organization wasn't true.' I spent 30 years in an organization believing we were a healthy community, and we aren't who I thought we were. I feel like I bought something and found out it wasn't real; it was plastic. I guess I so wanted us to be this loving, caring community of faith that I overlooked the signs that said we weren't.

"The pain is greatest where the relationship was deepest. I know there is a sort of unwritten rule in the state not to contact former executives. But still, there is a sadness, a painful sadness, about those close relationships with friends who served with me and who we walked in accountability with. I guess I thought our relationships were different. We'd said that wherever we were in life we would always be there for each other, that we would do that for our whole lives. And one of these brothers has never contacted me.

"What is happening in my heart these days? There are some good things and some challenges. So many things went wrong in the last two years. We started raising cattle to help make ends meet, but the buyers totally misrepresented the animals I was getting and it ended up being a money loser. I had the same experience being cheated while buying tires. I bought the gold package, with tire rotation and balancing and everything, so I thought it was all covered. But when I blew a tire a short time later I discovered that the gold package left out road hazard coverage, so I was out the whole cost of it.

"That was just one of dozens of similar miscues. Our son got hurt really bad on the farm and a bone was sticking out of his leg. God was amazingly good. In fact, he just got the cast off. But the day he got out of hospital my mother broke her hip. Then the doctor messed up her surgery and she had to have another operation three days later. There have been lots of areas in my life where I am scratching my head and saying, 'How did that happen?!?' It's the most random chaos I've ever experienced in my life. So my coping skills and trust in God are growing!

"Looking back, I think God was doing two things. First, I would have been tempted to stay in the cattle business if it was all working, and that wasn't the right place for me. Second, things don't bug me as much as they did. I used to get upset about small amounts of money, but when people cheat you out of $10,000 at a time… well, the rest seems pretty small by comparison.

"Part of what makes all this waiting uncomfortable is the financial strain. I realize that in the midst of it God has sustained us. But I have been a high-level, successful person, and when people ask what I am doing, I have nothing to say.

"So, where do we go next? I don't know. I want to spend time with my kids and grandkids. And I'd love to create relational events for pastors, to help them find God's next place when they feel the rug is pulled out from under them. Pastors used to ask me, 'What does a general do when he is no longer a general?' Many of them are afraid of becoming irrelevant, of being put out to pasture. Instead. I would also take them overseas on a spiritual journey in a fun way."

Jacob, my Good Soldier,

I salute you, faithful and fearless! The applause of heaven greets you in the triumphal procession winding through your heaven-home. Well done!

You still have a flesh wound from the last battle. You acted heroically, and a medal of honor awaits you, but first we need to treat your wound. Let go of your rifle, and let me escort you to the field hospital. Because of your strength and spiritual health, the wound of betrayal and disappointment is not life-threatening. However, it is still bleeding, and if we don't treat it, it will get worse. You are my concern now—I don't want to lose my best sergeant. So stand down, soldier, and we'll get you back in fighting shape ASAP.

You've been through a tough time. I know the loss of relationships hurt you more than the loss of position, and I am proud of you for that. You kept first things first. That was well done. You have taken care of the needs of others, and preserved the organization to fight another day. Now, would you allow me the privilege of taking care of you and dressing your wounds?

I'm not telling you to wait and not put yourself forward in ministry because I'm in any way displeased with you. No! I've put you on leave because it is the time for giving to you. I want to love you, heal you and have you by my side. Don't spend your leave time pining for battle—enjoy it. Enjoy your grandchildren, enjoy working with your hands and enjoy being alone with me.

You are on an extended leave, Jacob. The purpose is to be healed and loved. Did you notice all the little betrayals you've experienced with the cattle and the tires and your mother's surgery? I'm not trying to make life hard for you—but each of those things is poking at the wound, reminding you it is still there. It is good that you are learning not to let pain slow you down. You are learning well. But there is a bigger lesson: healing the wound is better than getting used to it. Put down your rifle, and let me heal you fully.

This one thought may help you. When I was on earth, I healed ten men of a life-threatening, humiliating disease, and only one ever came back to thank me. If they treat the general this way, won't they do the same to his sergeant? I know, it isn't fair or fun when the people you've loved don't repay the favor, but it is human nature. Let's take a walk sometime and talk about it. It does my heart good to be with a fellow soldier who has felt the same pain as I have.

I want you to understand more of what I have been doing in you in this season, so you can march in step with me. Your desire is to provide a place and a healing for pastors who have had the rug pulled out from them, and to restore vision by taking them overseas. As soon as you saw that picture I began to pull together the gear you'd need for the mission. The first order of business was to provide you with experiences that allow you to identify with their pain, and help them to trust you because you've been there. That step is mostly complete. Well done, soldier!

The second objective is for you to go through the healing process they also must embrace. The journey you are on is your combat training: I am giving you an inside look at the pain they must walk through and how to heal it. In the process, I'm teaching you the tools and skills you'll need to help them complete their mission. Learning to walk through financial strain in trust is a tool. Learning to identify sadness and disappointment and drain the wound is an ability you'll need. Waiting is an especially crucial skill. Your mission today is to pay attention to my healing process. Lean into it, observe it and take notes on how I am leading you to wholeness. Because once you have finished, I will assign you a company to take on the same journey.

The third goal is about faith and identity. The pastors your heart goes out to often struggle because their hearts are attached to ministry. They need the approval and significance ministering gives them to feel that they are valuable. You ask, "What does a general do when he is no longer a general?" Good—your heart is in just the right place. Because these men and women believe a general's worth is in his or her role, they believe they are nothing when their roles are stripped away. And they fear being put out to pasture.

Your job is to teach them different. And to teach them, you must first experience this: that I love my soldiers for who they are, for their companionship and for my image in them. Every soldier of mine is as glorious in retirement, marching in a Veteran's Day parade, as they ever were in the foxhole.

Knowing that in theory is not enough to move their hearts—so I am teaching you that truth in practice. Letting go of the role, the relationships that filled your heart and even your ability to make something happen or provide for yourself in order to let me be everything to you, That will make you powerful in your destiny. This season of your life is going to move you from being a foot soldier to driving a tank—an exponential increase in your firepower.

So don't fight the process! Do you feel you are sitting down instead of marching into battle, and so your worth is less? But I say tank drivers must go into battle sitting down! So sit and absorb the lesson, and put on my power. From now on instead of marching into battle carrying a 60-pound pack, you'll go in sitting—but with 60 tons of combat power at your command.

Don't worry, and don't wonder, because everything in your life is unfolding according to the battle plan. You are exceedingly valuable, incredibly significant and overflowingly loved. You are my soldier.

Your General,

Jesus

The OUTCOME

"I can remember exactly where I was sitting when I read the story," Jacob recalls. "It had a really positive impact. From those first two paragraphs, where the story said I was on 'extended leave,' it moved the situation from pain without purpose to purposeful pain. Truthfully, today I feel almost no pain over it. The story was an 'aha' moment that put things in a very different perspective.

"The idea of the one who came back to thank Jesus out of the ten who were healed also really impacted me. The thought that you help people and it doesn't come back to you… I had this epiphany, 'Well, if that happened to Jesus, why should I expect it to be any better for me?' So many people made no effort to contact me—people who I was sure that none of what happened with my position would change our relationship. That was such a painful disappointment for me that I was walking in this maze of negative emotions I couldn't escape from.

"At first I just hurt. There was no comfort, only more pain. That lasted for two years, with pain as a constant companion. These thoughts kept rolling around in my mind: I didn't leave as well as I could have and I didn't have the relationships I thought I had. It wasn't like I was paralyzed and couldn't work, but my mind kept returning to these covenant relationships. At the time when I got the story the pain was diminishing, but the confusion was still there. And the story helped bring some clarity to why I was where I was at.

"Looking back, I can see that I had a lot of idealistic distortions about who we were. I was just walking numbly through the pain of disillusionment, and I didn't have a place or a project to pour myself into to distract myself. So I had to cope with what was happening inside me instead of jumping into something new. If I had put all my energy into doing, I wouldn't have had to address my distorted expectations or the feelings of rejection that came from placing a hope in people and relationships that only belonged to God. I so had hoped to live a life that pleased both God and men, and with my leadership gifts I could easily have been pleasing people well in a new location.

"Instead, I wasn't doing anything. I wasn't impressing myself or anyone else. I had to see my emotional and spiritual self in a mirror, in an emotionally and spiritually naked way. This situation put me in a position where I had to look at myself at a different level. This was God's journey—and I didn't choose it.

"But it was worth it. It has brought a quiet confidence. Negative things don't rattle me like they once did. My fierce sense that my fellow man would treat me justly—well, after being treated unjustly on so many levels, I don't feel a need any more to address most of the injustices that have happened to me. There is injustice in the world, and it will all be okay.

"And I am more confident in my relationship with the Lord. In all the chaos and disorder, there really does appear to be something pretty orderly about life. There is a nice picture emerging, although I am not sure what that picture is!

"Out of all of that chaos, I am starting my thesis on church transformation and all these doors are opening. I am planning a creative degree program to train young ministry leaders debt-free. The pieces are all there. And God is inspiring me to write. Out of everything that looked crazy and chaotic, I am finding joy and health in writing things that will help transform churches."

Chapter 5:
OUTWARD VS. INWARD

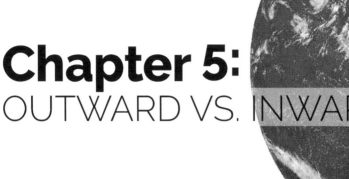

"And we know that God causes all things to work together for good to those who love God, to those who are called according to His purpose."

(Rom. 8:28)

One of the big questions you face when you work with people's painful stories is, "Did God cause all this crap?" How do you reconcile God's sovereignty with his goodness in a world filled with evil? Or to put it more personally, how can God be good to me when my life circumstances are so bad?

Romans 8:28 gives a piece of the answer. For those who love God and who've answered his call, any circumstance we experience is leveraged for our good. Let's take a closer look at what that passage means.

An excellent starting place is the word for "good" in Greek, which is *agathon*. Agathon can have different shades of meaning, but I believe the best fit here is the most common definition: that of inward goodness or good character. So Romans 8:28 asserts that all your circumstances work to produce *inward* goodness in you. They work to shape your heart so you look like Jesus.

The passage doesn't mean, "everything will turn out good," in the sense that if your car dies God will give you a new one, or if you lose your keys you will find them. It is not a promise of a happy ending in this life. The "good" that God causes is *not a change of your circumstances but a change of your heart.*

Customer SERVICE

Years ago, I got a nasty and unexpected call from a collection agency. They claimed my merchant account (used to run credit cards) was still active and I owed them three months' worth of service fees. I explained that I'd called and cancelled in January, three months before, so they apologized and hung up—only to call me again two months later. Now they said I owed them *five* months' worth, which was $500. At this point I got ticked off. I called the company I'd had the account with, but they claimed they had no record of my call, and treated me as if I was trying to shirk a legitimate debt.

That began a two-month odyssey through the bowels of customer service, talking to endless reps and managers. I spent a total of eight hours on the phone, sent eight faxes and 20-some e-mails before they finally discovered weeks later that the gal who had taken my original call back in January (it was now August) quit that same day, and never put her notes about canceling the account into the billing database. So it wasn't my fault after all! But the manager refused to apologize or offer any compensation for my ordeal. To make matters worse, they never removed the charge from my credit report! That mistaken bill showed up as an unpaid debt for years.

So, how is God working all things for good in that situation? He didn't protect me from injustice. He didn't pay me back for me for the time I wasted talking to reps who didn't believe me. And he didn't work a miracle to clean up my credit report, either. So just what *did* he do?

About halfway through customer service odyssey, I began to get convicted about how nasty I was being on the phone to low-level customer service people who weren't even responsible for my problem. So I gritted my teeth and said, "Okay, Lord, I will try to treat them well." And I did (although a couple times I almost bit my tongue off).

So I learned a valuable lesson about how to treat people through that experience. Is that what Romans 8:28 means? Actually, no. There's much more. I was telling that story one day years later when all of the sudden it dawned on me: my primary ministry as a coach was over the phone. I was spending 20 or even 30 hours a week on the phone with people, and just before I began in that career, God was dealing with me about my phone manner!

That changed the whole story. It was no longer about the outward injustice, but the inward formation. That's the Outward versus Inward reframe. Instead of seeing the situation as injustice, or even about learning a good, practical lesson in how to treat people, I experienced my Good Father forming me into the man I needed to be to fulfill my destiny! I didn't even realize what he was doing. So I had to repent then and there about having such a crappy attitude when he was just trying to love me well.

God's OPTIONS

There were four things God could have done in that situation. One, he could have *protected me* from bad things ever happening to me. Two, he could have *restored to me* the time and energy I lost (and cleared my credit report.) Three, he could have *taught me* a valuable lesson about how to treat people. Or four, he could have *formed me* into the person I needed to be to fulfill my destiny. What most of us ask for are the first and the second things: God's protection and restoration for our outward circumstances. That's what I wanted, too. Instead God gave me the best: forming me to be like him. And in heaven, the rewards for being conformed to the image of Christ are incalculable.

So did God cause that whole painful situation to get at my heart? No, I don't think so. I believe what Romans 8:28 says. *Things* happen, and God turns them to our advantage. He is so big he can take even what others do to damage us and turn it to our good (see Gen. 50:20). The ultimate example is the cross. The enemy thought he was killing his rival, the only Son of God, but Father leveraged that ultimate evil to the ultimate good, the redemption of all creation.

Father is so amazingly adept at turning evil on its head that when you see the beauty that comes out of it, you'd almost believe he caused the whole thing from the beginning. The word "leveraged" is a better description of God's activity than "caused." He is not the source of evil, suffering or difficulty, but instead leverages whatever happens to us for our good. And that good is not outward accomplishment, but inward formation leading to our heavenly glory.

In the stories of Kathy and Marianne that follow, prepare to be amazed as you watch Father take brokenness and evil and intricately weave them into good.

Nothing WILL BE MISSED

"Every good and perfect gift is from above, coming down from the Father of the heavenly lights, who does not change like shifting shadows" (James 1:17 NIV).

Kathy Ward is a 57-year-old mother of three, with the type of sunny disposition that comes from shining through the rain instead of maneuvering around it. She's the kind of person you just naturally count on to be solid, who picks everyone else up and who is a stabilizing presence.

"I became a serious Christian and went after God starting with my senior year of college," Kathy begins. "For nine years before I got married I was on staff for several different college student ministries. College kids are alive with possibility, hope and loaded with passion. I loved working with them. Because I felt called to ministry, I studied for a master's degree in Christian education and counseling. I felt so alive! My days were filled with leading Bible studies, one-on-one discipleship and meetings. Whenever the doors at church were open, I was there.

"I married my Steve in 1990 when we were both 30, and shortly after got pregnant. I had always said that I wanted to have enough kids for at least a basketball team, so we thought we'd better get busy. We were beyond excited to bring a new life into our happy world. As we prayed over my growing baby bump each night my excitement grew. Her little life would soon completely change the world we had known. In 1991 Kait was born—and our lives turned upside down.

"It was a very traumatic birth. After 35 hours in labor she finally arrived blue and not breathing, and was rushed away in a panic to the ICU. Those long, aching moments after the delivery were awful. Instead of a greatly anticipated time of bonding skin to skin, I was left with only empty arms and worry. The doctors brought her back to life, but it would be three days before I even got to hold her. Feeling God's nearness kept my hope alive as I looked achingly through the glass at our bruised and badly swollen little girl. We thought the drama was over—but it was really just beginning.

"We finally brought our new daughter home a week later.

One of the first discoveries was that Kait was highly sensitive to sounds. We found it impossible to go church or any public setting where a sudden laugh, a clink of glass or loud music could cause Kait to hold her breath, arch her back and ultimately vomit. She was unable to make eye contact at all. Smiles, cooing, following movement, and other basic newborn behaviors were strangely absent. Kait was like an alien from another planet. It was a very lonely time as our world continually grew smaller and we were completely consumed by this little life.

"Though I felt cut off from the world and from our community at church, God was doing a deep work inside us. He was breaking our religious belief that we were only as good as our church attendance or the good things we were doing. Faith became simple and Jesus became a lot more real to us.

"I began learning how to have really honest conversations with the Lord. I deeply value peace and am not one to confront at all, so I had never dreamed of conversing with God in such a combative tone. I was bawling my eyes out at church, saying, 'Lord, what is this? Why did this happen?' There was no reply. But between Kleenexes I began to get a sense of his presence, which made me quiet myself. 'This is my best for you,' I heard him clearly say. That made no sense to me at all at the time, and still didn't answer my question: 'Will you heal her?'

"At six months Kait contracted a respiratory condition and we lived for four months at the hospital again. My feelings ranged from angry to angrier. I raged at God, feeling betrayed and abandoned. I had played by the rules and had been the good girl—but what had been my reward? Exhausted and worn out, I finally came to the end of myself and found the One who stood up in my little, almost-capsized boat and spoke peace to my wave-tossed soul. I finally gave up my right to understand, and made peace with the mystery. The storm in my soul was over, for now.

"Eventually the doctors delivered their diagnosis that Kait was severely mentally retarded and deeply autistic. As we struggled for the next breath, I wondered what this meant for our lives. Over the next few years my momma's heart was ever waiting for that first syllable that sounded like 'ma-ma.' But the sounds never came.

"There have been seasons where I felt like God was saying, 'Pray!' So, we would pray hard, but healing didn't come. And then we'd go through seasons where we were just doing life, trying to get through the next day. And then we'd go through another season where we felt an urgency to pray, pray, pray. That has been the back and forth of the whole thing, doing what he says just because he said to do it, even when we didn't understand. Over the years I've made my peace with it. I don't know the mystery, but I will dance with it. I don't always have the heart anymore to pray for her to be healed, but Jesus told me, 'I've heard the prayers you don't even have the heart to pray.' Having to pursue him through all of this has changed me a million times over.

"When she was three we took Kait to a treatment center in Philadelphia where there was a high, high level of hope that if you could follow their therapeutic regime, she could experience healing and she could improve. So we began a huge therapeutic program that started literally from the moment we woke to the time we put Kait to bed. There were over 100 people involved in the day-to-day operation of her therapy. We rarely left the house for those two years. We really didn't need to go to church during that time, because our church came to us! It was incredibly rich but utterly exhausting. We finally felt we just couldn't do it—we couldn't keep up that pace anymore. And we wanted more kids, which was terrifying at the same time. But we had such a peace about growing our family that we went ahead.

"Today, Kait is a little firecracker—short and small, with not an ounce of body fat. Typically, she's very happy. She's like one big muscle, and loves large-motor activities like running or kicking balls. We've gone through nine trampolines in her 24 years of jumping!

"But cognitively, she measures about three years old. She doesn't understand the danger of streets or strangers. She has a compulsive drive to pick up objects and eat them, and needs help with the simple, basic skills like dressing, bathing and toileting.

"We have been greatly blessed that we have gotten a grant for her care. I've developed a training program and we've been able to keep together a team to work with her. One of those friends has stayed on our team for 20 years! People on the team spend four hours at a time with her.

"Kait has things she does to serve the community as well. For example, she goes and collects people's trash. I wanted her to get out and have places in the community that know her. She is pretty blessed to have two or three people a day who come and spend quality time with her.

"What is my greatest moment with Kait? That's an interesting question. I'm not sure I've had one specific moment. A relationship with Kait is different than most and far more difficult because she has no language. Moments with Kait often feel familiar and quite mundane as her days are filled with a constantly, repeating routine.

"Some of my sweetest times are when I wake her up and put a kiss on her face and see her eyes. There is not a lot said. But there is a sweetness and knowing and trusting—she kisses me back and grabs my hand. Most of the time Kait doesn't like a lot of touch, and I am a real touchy person. So those little moments before bed and when I get her up—those are my two special times with her. Those are the only occasions she really lets me touch her.

"I love those little moments with Kait and am thankful for them, but it makes me wish for the ability to have a special moment. That's still my biggest unanswered question. Will I ever see her healed? Will I ever hear her talk or see her look at me and say, 'Momma'?

"But I'm thankful that I have her. I've learned that gratefulness is a choice. You have to recognize it and name it and choose it. Because I've always had an awareness that things could be much worse, I am thankful for what I have. And staying fresh in that, staying aware of it, is important. There is a deep presence of the Lord when I stay in the place of gratefulness. I am not always there, but I can get there.

"One thing that's a big deal to me in this is that I feel Father's approval and his affirmation that I have done well. He's happy with it, and happy with me—and that makes me happy.

"I can remember when having other people's approval was a big, big deal to me. I think the longing for approval started with my dad. He was a big, dominant, in-charge figure in our home. It was all-important for me, the first born, to be the good girl to win the elusive approval that I desperately sought. In tennis, even in getting my master's degree—I was partly doing that to make my becoming a Christian (which upset my dad, who was so intellectual) more palatable to him, because it would make me seem more intellectual than emotional. Gaining his approval seems to lace my every action.

"The home my sister I were raised in was a strong Irish Catholic family. The work ethic was high and chores were a central part of the rhythm of our home. After dinner dad would sit at the table, pat his lap with his hands and say, 'The hugging spot is open.' The race was on! Whoever got their chores done first and done well got to sit in the hugging spot. For you see, there was only ONE spot! It deeply reinforced in me that I could win approval by being the good girl.

"My sister wouldn't play that game, but I loved it. I would do whatever I could to get to sit in that hugging spot. But the love I got was conditional and hard-earned. I had to be approved by dad to get that loving touch I so craved.

"I wanted to be understood and approved by my friends also, so I spent a lot of energy making sure people knew what I doing and why. As a new believer there were so many ways to work out my approval. Leading a study, going to as many meetings as possible, or volunteering were all ways to get my need met.

"But now it is okay when people can't understand me—when even our closest friends don't fully grasp what our lives are like. So much of what we have to do day in and day out people don't see. That's why God's approval is so important, because he is the one who has seen it all. It is enough that we feel his okay."

Dearest Kathy, my favorite,

Daughter, my peace rests on you. It rests there because I love to give it, but also because of you. You have come to the place that all humans yearn for and yet very few attain: that I am truly all you need. You have taken your greatest desire (approval) and put it fully in my hands. You have known me and my presence, and it has become enough for you, even in the valley of the shadow. No person or circumstance can take that security away from you.

Now, there is an accomplishment of great worth to heaven! You will enjoy the fruit of that victory all the days of your life. Kathy, you have become all that I created you to be, and I celebrate it. And you have accomplished the mission I created you to perform, and I am well pleased.

So do not let your heart say, "But Jesus, all I have accomplished is small and hidden. I wanted to change the world." Because I say, "You have!"

Remember when your child was young and you led a ministry of 100 staff to serve her? You put everything you had to give into that ministry. The world sees your accomplishment as small because it was all targeted at one person. But we measure impact in a completely different way in heaven. To us, leading a staff of 100 carries the same reward whether the mission is one person or ten thousand.

You see, from heaven's perspective, Father's plans will be and already have been completed. Nothing can stop his will, and nothing can add to it. Therefore, you are not rewarded according to how much you helped the plan along, because it will be completed whether you helped it or not. Your great contribution to heaven is not your work, for goodness sake! No, Father's pleasure is found in the largeness of your heart in doing it. It is the depth of your surrender and the height of your love that we value, not the number of people you reach or the size of your organization. Size is no obstacle to Father (and the sizes you humans dream in are all impossibly tiny to him anyway). But fellowship with a human heart that has freely chosen to love and serve the One—now, that we count as value beyond measure!

And the joy and gratitude you maintain in your giving is extraordinary. It literally lights up heaven with song and celebration!

Everyday happiness on earth is a flickering candle, a dim light that fades into shadow in eternity. In heaven all things become their true selves. Much of what earth calls happiness is a faint shade of gray to us—a dry leaf or the ashes of a dead fire. But this happiness you have, the gratitude you have chosen at great cost in the crucible of adversity—that happiness bursts into a full flame of glory in eternity! It becomes a joy that lasts and even grows forever. Know daughter, that what you have chosen for my sake you keep for eternity.

And still my best for you gets even better, my beautiful one! In heaven, your daughter will be perfect, not just in body but also in mind. Kait will remember, with perfect cognition, every moment with you on earth. Her spirit is now alive to all those moments—it is merely trapped inside a body that cannot communicate what she is experiencing. In heaven you will get to relive each moment with her true self. You will experience her life through her eyes, and she through yours, until you fully know and fully understand each other. And every touch, every word, every loving response, every tear of joy that you missed out on on earth you will live out fully together in heaven.

I have willed it and it shall be done. You will have more love, more joy and more gratitude to share than you ever would have known if Kait had been born whole, because the weakness of her body has called out an extraordinary love in you. And in that moment you will turn to me and say, "Jesus, now that I know the whole story, I can truly and finally say: this really was your best for me." Those are the moments I live for!

I have one more secret to share with you, my favored one, just to show you how wide and deep Father's plans for you go. When you were growing up, you experienced a father who loved you, but made speaking your love language of touch (in the hugging spot) conditional upon your performance. You were bound, unable to receive the loving touch you sought except through being good. But your Father in heaven has fully redeemed you from that bondage, and the evidence is this: you are able to love beautifully the daughter who is unable to touch you.

When you have the power to give that which you most lacked, and give it freely, then you are free indeed. Father has arranged it so that your own actions demonstrate your freedom every day of your life. So each time you give Kait the love that dwells in you, a love that expects nothing in return, find joy in this: that you are experiencing the fruit of your redemption. And to top it off, you are also displaying to the principalities and powers in the heavenly places the true depth of Father's power and wisdom. So you aren't just fulfilling his will on earth, you are accomplishing it in heaven as well!

My dearest Kathy, you know what I am about to say, and yet I will say it again and again: I am pleased in you, I approve you, and I love you forever and ever and ever!

Your big brother,

Jesus

P.S. The hugging spot is still wide open. But come quickly—I can only hug an infinite number of people at one time!

The OUTCOME

"What did my God-story mean to me?" Kathy asks wistfully. "I felt like there were so many places in my story where I had a head-knowledge of the truth, but as I experienced it through this letter from Jesus all the lights came on! The truth that he celebrates over me because I know him and love his presence struck at my deepest heart. It became concrete and real as I literally saw Jesus dancing with Father over me. I was undone. It was no longer just something I believed. It went deeper and connected in my heart.

"Jesus said that I had accomplished the mission he had created for me to perform, and that he was pleased. There is absolutely nothing in the world that could make my heart leap out of my chest more than to hear this! It felt so intimate. It made me weep to think of the God of heaven approving of me like this.

"When I read the line about me leading a ministry of 100 staff I started looking around the room to try and get someone to change that line. Had the storywriter misunderstood me? I thought back and rehearsed what I had told him, trying to remember, knowing that I would never have said that. As I sat pondering that one line, I felt a gentle nudge to read on, and then saw that it was not the size of contribution or accomplishment but the heart with which it was done that honored him. The Spirit concurred in me. I was undone again.

"That God will never waste anything has been a theme in my life, but this redemption was outrageous. To think that in heaven I would get to relive with Kait every milestone she never passed, hear every loving word she never spoke, sing with her every happy song she loved—all that and more she will receive, and I along with her! I am undone again as I begin to imagine all the things that I would get to share with her on that side of eternity: every touch I couldn't give, every time I had to restrain her instead of lovingly comfort her, every time I wanted to cuddle and hug her but couldn't, every moment I wanted to ask her how she was feeling or where it hurt but got no answer, and every time I wanted to ask her how her day was but couldn't. It lightens my everyday burden to think on heaven's redemptive reality and the outrageous extent of it.

"There was a divine reversal in my God-story that blew me away. I had gotten a word from the Lord in the very early days that Kait was 'his best for me.' The word was hard to understand but I felt so certain it had come from him. In my letter I begin to understand the depth of Kait's redemption, and the faithfulness of God to bring about more love and joy in our situation. I perceive his ultimate purpose in changing my heart to become more like his. It was so intimate. I felt so known deeply and loved. I have to end by proclaiming that, 'Yes, God, all this truly has been your best for me.'

"Then lastly, it was amazing to see how God took my desperate need for approval and worked into my life the healing and wholeness I had always longed for—from my place of greatest suffering—and brought everything together for me out of his intense, relentless love for me! That which had produced in me a lifetime of shame was his delight to heal. That was a touch so deep. I was known in the deepest places where only I could see, and I was loved completely.

"But that's not all! Beyond my imagining, the idea that my loving actions could display to principalities and powers in heaven the Father's power and wisdom is incredible. These things give a value to my life that is incomprehensible. Understanding heaven this way has changed how I view my everyday life."

Contact Kathy at Kathy@HeavensPerspective.com

Deeper IN HIS LOVE

Raised in a Christian home, Marianne prayed to receive Jesus at a Bible camp when she was only nine years old. Hearing a missionary speak, she thought, "Wow! That's cool! I know God wants me to tell people about him, and as a missionary I would get to do that all the time!" So at 24 years old she applied and got accepted to go to the mission field.

"During the training process with the mission board," she recalls, "a speaker came and talked to us about Africa, and I felt that was where I was supposed to go. Typically, it took a single woman 24 months to raise enough support to be sent out to the field, but it only took me twelve. I had friends call me up out of the blue offering support, and even had pastors I didn't know call me who had heard about what I was doing.

"The missionary kids I spoke to told me that the biggest thing they wanted out on the field was more books. I believed God wanted me to bring a library for the missionary kids as well as an IBM Selectric typewriter. Through a sale I was able to purchase 3,500 books for only ten dollars, and shortly after was given the typewriter by my employer! God's miraculous provision for both my support and the library were huge confirmations, and would be important down the road in knowing that God had called me to the mission field.

"Arriving in Africa I was looking forward to getting to work. There were three other couples stationed where I was going, and the couple leading our group had been in the field for 35 years. I was so excited to learn from them and had the utmost respect for them. Little did I know that they did not share in my excitement.

"At first they seemed very pleasant towards me, but after a few months I could start to tell something was off. I found out later from one of the other couples that they had been praying for six couples from my training class to join them, but instead all they got was one single woman—me. They told me my kind didn't make it out there, and then they set out to make their words come true.

"I'd applied with the mission board to raise money for a car, but this couple wrote the board and said that it was too dangerous for a single woman and that they would drive me around instead. Then when I would ask for a ride they would complain about what a burden it was to have single woman on staff. So I began walking and taking public transportation instead, which made them even more angry.

"The other missionary couples used to send their house helpers to the market to buy their food. I thought it was important to learn the language, and so I would go to the market myself. I began to pick up the language and it got to the point where I could barter with the locals and they treated me like one of their own. They even gave me the name 'Wanjiro,' which basically meant 'white black woman.'

"That infuriated the older couple even more. They said I was wasting my time learning the language because there was always someone around who could translate. I found out later that they wrote letters back to the mission board telling them that I was lazy and that I was spending time on things that didn't matter. They also wrote that I should live closer to where they were so that they could keep an eye on me, as they suspected I might even be on drugs.

"One of my jobs while I was in Africa was to teach in the Bible institute there. I would teach people in leadership from the church who wanted to learn more about God. The first thing that I taught was how to share a salvation message with someone and the concept that God loves you.

"This got the other missionaries really upset. They told me 'God used to love the world, but he doesn't anymore. It's theologically wrong to say God loves you.'

"The tradition that I come from is a very strict and angry form of Christianity. We would only talk about God the Father. My perception was that He was an angry Father that was going to send everyone to hell. God loved us enough to send Jesus to die for us, but that was where his love ended: at the cross. Now, his wrath resides on each one of us until we are saved.

"Growing up I was taught that emotions were bad and that love was an action, not a feeling. God didn't experience an emotional side to love. He intervened in our lives because it's what was best for us and it was the right thing to do, not because he actually felt anything towards us. So the more I talked about

God's love for us, the more those missionaries rejected me."

"After two-and-a-half years the stuff that had been going on behind my back finally started to come to light. At one of our field council meetings the older couple said they didn't think it was right to have single women on the field. We went around the circle and voted and the votes came back four to three agreeing that a single woman should no longer be allowed in the field.

"I was devastated. Just like that, my dream of being a life-long missionary ended. With so much rejection and the feeling that I couldn't do anything right, I became suicidal. I had a large bottle of nail polish remover in my bathroom that I looked at every morning, and tried to work up the courage to end things. It became my little bottle of hope as a way out.

"I felt divorced by God. I wanted answers. I couldn't defend myself because I didn't know what was being said about me, so I thought he would defend me. But he didn't. Everything I believed about God was crumbling down around me.

"I cried out asking him what was going on, but all I heard in return was silence. For the three years I was in Africa, he was silent. Even though my church taught that God had stopped speaking when the Bible was finished being written, I always felt like I could hear from him. I had found comfort in that, but now he was silent, and I felt abandoned and alone.

"I was so angry. I was angry that those people got to stay on the mission field and that I had to go home. I thought that for sure God would expose everything that they had done and that they would have to leave and I would get to stay, but that didn't happen. I got to the point where I was even questioning God's existence. It was easier for me to believe that there was no God than to believe there was a God who could allow all of this in my life.

"When I got home from Africa I sat down with a pastor who had a master's degree in counseling to help me process through some of the pain I had experienced. But after about five minutes he exclaimed, "Oh, you're Jim Smith's daughter. You'll be fine," and just waived his hand and dismissed me.

"A few years later, I got married and began attending a

non-denominational church. They offered something called Stephen's ministry, where someone comes alongside you and walks you through a dark time in your life. Instead of giving you answers, they listen to you and love you through the process.

"One day while I was in training for that ministry we were speaking about the healing power of God's word, and how simply reading his word over someone can be healing. The leader began reading Psalm 23, and as she did I saw a vivid image of Jesus, standing right in front of me. His eyes locked on mine, and as she read the words of Psalm 23 I could hear him speak the same words over me in Swahili. In Africa I had memorized Psalm 23 for a language exam, and so I had those words in my head. But now, as Jesus spoke them they began to penetrate my heart.

"That was a huge breakthrough moment for me, because Jesus had never been part of the equation before. I was always taught that he was basically just someone who lived a long time ago. I didn't realize that I could have an actual relationship with him in the present. Ten years after I left Africa I met Jesus in that room, and he began a healing journey that is still happening today."

My Dear, Sweet Love, Wanjiro,

You are so precious to me! I love you so much and I'm overjoyed that you're here with me now. That's right Marianne, you bring joy to my heart. As much as I love filling your heart with joy I also love how you fill mine. You fill it to overflowing. When I'm with you I'm so full I feel like I could burst!

I'm so sorry that I felt so far away during your time in Africa. But I was never distant. I've never left you. I will always be with you. When you felt like I was far away, the truth is I was holding you close, protecting you—so close in fact that it was hard to hear my voice at times because I was wrapping my arms around you, pulling you right to my chest. I was protecting and defending you the best way I know how, not by raining down fire and brimstone on your enemies, but by enveloping you in my love. You were raised in a tradition that kept me at an angry distance, so when injustice touched you it made my voice of love hard to hear.

You see Marianne, when insults were being hurled at you when you spoke up about my love, it wasn't you that was offending them, it was me. I sent you for the express purpose of offending them, in answer to their prayers for more. In their minds they thought that more meant more people (the six couples they prayed for), but I wanted to give them something so much better: more depth, more relationship—more me! All prayers for more are prayers for more of me. And so I sent you, because you knew how to love me and talk to me, and that was what I wanted for them. My darling, I never stop loving even those who are stuck outside of love. And just as far as I went to redeem them when they were angry and had lost their way, that far and more I will go for you as well, my beloved!

Although it didn't feel like it, you were so close to my heart that you couldn't help but start to share my love with those around you. To your leaders it was repulsive, because they thought that my love ended at the cross. But the cross was just the beginning. The locals saw more truly: what you did was attractive to them because your love—learning their language, going to the market, caring for people well—bore the fragrance of heaven.

Marianne I need you to hear this: well done! I'm so proud of how you handled your time in Africa. Your prayer was always that you would be able to share my truth accurately, and that you wouldn't misrepresent me. You did, and you continue to do that so well. Although your leaders didn't respond to my invitation to change, our act of offering love to them is cherished eternally here in my Kingdom, and will stand as a memorial before me forever in the honor and bliss of heaven.

Know this as well: I also leveraged this situation to help you become all you were born to be. To carry the message that I am a God of love and grace, you actually have to experience those things deeply yourself. Did you know that grace means unmerited favor? In order to truly experience grace, you first have to lose all of your merit. You were in a merit-based system, and by having your merit taken away—although it was painful—you were able to truly experience my grace in your life.

You believed rightly at that time that you were called to be a missionary. That was well done. But your mission is not so much to a people or to a place, but to be my love and grace to all you meet. I was working to prepare you for your true mission: to be my hands of love and feet of grace wherever you go in this world. And you did it! You went deeper in my love. Oh, how I love to overwhelm you with my love!

Daughter, in heaven there is no such thing as time, because heaven exists in an eternal now. Everything is happening in constant present. That means your love encounter with me when I read Psalm 23 over you in Swahili is just as present for me right now as it was many years ago. So come with me and let me read those sweet words to you again!

Bwana Mchungaji Wetu

Bwana ndiye mchungaji wangu, sitapungukiwa na kitu. Katika malisho ya majani mabichi hunilaza, kando ya maji ya utulivu huniongoza, huhuisha nafsi yangu. Huniongoza katika njia za haki kwa ajili ya jina lake.

Psalm 23 (RSV)

The Lord is my shepherd, I shall not want; he makes me lie down in green pastures. He leads me beside still waters; he restores my soul. He leads me in paths of righteousness for his name's sake. Even though I walk

Naam, nijapopita katikati ya bonde la uvuli wa mauti, sitaogopa mabaya, kwa maana wewe upo pamoja nami, rungu yako na fimbo yako vyanifar- iji. Waandaa meza mbele yangu machoni pa watesi wangu. Umeni- paka mafuta kichwani pangu, kikombe changu kinafurika. Hakika wema na fadhili zitanifuata siku zote za maisha yangu, nami nitakaa nyumbani mwa Bwana milele.

through the valley of the shadow of death, I fear no evil; for thou art with me; thy rod and thy staff, they comfort me. Thou preparest a table before me in the presence of my enemies; thou anointest my head with oil, my cup overflows. Surely goodness and mercy shall follow me all the days of my life; and I shall dwell in the house of the Lord forever.

Marianne, I love you. I have never left you. I will always be with you. From before time began you were set apart to share me with the world and to bring purpose to the purposeless. And there is no one I would rather be doing that with than you!

Your Good Shepherd,

Jesus

The OUTCOME

"Reading my rewritten story was another huge step in my healing journey," Marianne recounts passionately. "During my encounter with Jesus speaking Psalm 23 over me, and when I reread it in this story, the portion that stood out the most was where he says, 'Yea though I walk through the valley of the shadow of death…thou art with me.' In Swahili it says the equivalent of, 'You are there in that place with me.' When Jesus first spoke to me I felt like he was saying that he was there in that place with me in Africa. However, this time I felt he was saying that he was there in that place of pain with me. As I read those words, I was overwhelmed with comfort and joy.

"I'd always wanted the truth of what happened to come out so that I could be vindicated over those people that hurt me so much. It bothered me that no one ever found out what they did. But when I read that he was protecting me the best way that he knew how, by enveloping me in his love, that shifted things. The point wasn't for him to punish or to choose sides; the point was for him to show me love in the midst of my pain.

"Growing up and going through what I did on the mission field, I had a head knowledge that God loved me (at least at some point), but it never penetrated my heart. I can see now that in his love he took me through what he did to uproot what I had been taught and prepare the soil of my heart to actually experience his love. Had he tried to show me sooner I don't think I would have been open to it, because my belief system wouldn't have allowed it.

"So if I could tell people one thing from my story, it would be the value of actually experiencing the love of Jesus. His love is not just an unfeeling action. There's a lot of emotion that goes along with it. Experiencing his love in my heart—as well as the joy and peace that come with it—as opposed to just knowing it in my head has changed everything for me. You don't have to wait until heaven to experience it. He wants you to have it today!"

Contact Marianne at Marianne@HeavensPerspective.com

Chapter 6:
HEAVEN VS. EARTH

"For my thoughts are not your thoughts, neither are your ways my ways, says the Lord. For as the heavens are higher than the earth, so are my ways higher than your ways and my thoughts than your thoughts"

(Is. 55:8-9 RSV).

Heaven operates by an entirely different set of rules than earth. It's the upside-down, inside-out Kingdom. So to truly understand your story and what it means, you have reframe it according to the rules of heaven.

Take the Beatitudes. They are heaven's rules for rewarding what we experience on earth. Are you living from hand-to-mouth these days, just barely eking by? Guess what—you have an obscenely rich relative who just bequeathed you an entire country in heaven! Have you mourned the untimely death of a child or spouse? Jesus is going to take you in his lap and person-ally wipe the tears from your eyes in heaven, where comfort is beyond earth's wildest imagining. Have you been taken advantage of in life because you weren't willing to push and fight to get your share? Well, the share heaven freely gives you is going to be huge—the entire *planet!*

God's whole reward system is out of this world. For instance, "He who receives a prophet because he is a prophet shall receive a prophet's reward" (Mt. 10:41 RSV). Let me translate that into modern English: "If you let a missionary on leave stay in your house for a night, you'll receive the same reward that missionary gets for a *lifetime* of service." Come on—really? If you help someone a little bit you share the reward they receive for their whole life?[1] Read it again: that's literally what it says. God's reward system is *crazy!*

Set up chairs for the worship gathering and everything that happens in the building that night is credited to your account. Send money to an orphanage and every one of those orphans will be in the parade welcoming you to heaven. Empower a fellow Christian in her career and all she accomplishes in the workplace from then on will be credited to your account. When a child grows up to accomplish great things for God, his babysitters also share in his full reward (wouldn't you love to have been Billy Graham's babysitter). Do you see now why, "whoever wishes to become great among you shall be your servant" (Mt. 20:26)? A ministry leader receives the reward of his or her own ministry, but those who serve in the background share the reward of *every* ministry they serve. Father rejoices in his reward system, because it connects our hearts and multiplies our joy as we share each others' glory.

Laws OF HEAVEN

God's reward system is one example of how the laws of heaven differ from those of earth. Here's another. On earth, justice means you get what you deserve. "An eye for an eye, a tooth for a tooth" is the foundation of humanity's legal systems. But in heav-

---

1   *That's the message of the parable about the laborers in the vineyard (see Mt. 20:1-16). God gave the latecomers who worked only an hour the same reward as those who worked all day in the hot sun, just because he likes being extravagantly good to us.*

en the law is that you always get *better* than you deserve. You don't get what is coming to you, you get what is coming to Jesus.

On earth, when you give something to another person, you no longer have it. But in heaven, every gift is multiplied, and the giver as well as the receiver both have it in full (it was this quality of heaven Jesus drew on when he multiplied the loaves and fishes). On earth, we choose between good and evil, while in heaven all choices point toward God.

Many of the relationship rules in Scripture are there to teach us how to live on earth as we will in heaven. For instance, New Testament leaders taught and modeled that we should live openly and authentically with each other. On earth, that's a choice we learn to make; but in the direct, spirit-to-spirit communion of heaven, hiding behind a mask will literally be impossible.

This next set of stories show how the laws of heaven govern God's activity on earth. Study the ways of God in dealing with his children, and you'll learn how heaven functions. You can even ask Jesus questions about it (he likes talking about his home). The more you know of heaven, the more you'll see God on earth.

One THING I DO

At 61, Jody Trudeau is a life-long missionary with a call to pioneer and encourage pioneers. After being ejected from a country he loved and had spent much of his life in for preaching the gospel, he found a way to continue to give by coaching overseas missionaries from the U.S. The life message Father has built into him is, "Apart from God I can do nothing, but with God nothing is impossible."

"The last three years have been ones of loss and sadness," Jody recounts. "My wife calls it 'Hell on earth.' Some really hard events triggered the loss of our home, bankruptcy and a sense of failure. It was like a sinking ship where we had to say, 'It's time to get in the lifeboat and move on.' My biggest question in it all is, 'Lord, what's this all been about? Where were you when my son was being sexually abused?'

"Our son Alain had had a year of difficult times as he was transitioning to a new school. It was only at the end of the year it came to light that he had been the victim of serious bullying and sexual abuse from an older child—a kid we had trusted. We got a call from the mom of one of the other children. Her son had been abused and it happened to others. So my wife Nichole spoke to Alain, then I went in and talked to him, and the details slowly dribbled out over the next two or three days. Our son's best friends confirmed that it had happened, starting when he was eight and lasting almost a year. Ultimately, criminal charges were filed by the parents of several of the other kids and the older child was convicted, but given a fairly light sentence.

"We were blindsided. In shock and disbelief, we didn't know what to feel or believe. We were trying to protect Alain and make sure it didn't happen to anyone else, and we were numb—just trying to survive. It was only later on that it started to really affect us. We were deeply upset and angry, and felt betrayed by a kid we trusted and by the system. When our older sons heard of it they were very shaken and angry, too.

"The following year Nichole was still under a lot of stress, and had a major health event. It appeared to be a heart attack, and we ended up making three trips to the ER. She never got a firm diagnosis, but her condition prevented her from going back to her job, and she finally resigned. Without her paycheck we were gradually going under. We finally concluded that to recover her health we needed to leave that stressful situation and leave the area. But the local economy was collapsing, we were under water on our house, and the only possible way to leave was to let our home go and file for bankruptcy. We tried every way around it, but nothing worked. We finally moved back to her hometown in Louisiana last summer, where we are living in an office in a commercial building that Nichole's father converted into an apartment for us. We've decided to locate here long term, but we are still in transition, and we can't have a home.

"Nichole and the whole family are in a much better place now. Her health is far more stable, but she still deals with a lot of fatigue. Living here has been great for Alain, with new friends, a great school and a lot of affirmation. He is the only kid at home now, so he gets a lot more attention from us. We see a level of confidence and security in him that that shows that he is in a good place. He feels like it is done and in the past, and doesn't have to worry about that happening again.

"My own response to it all was to focus on helping my family. I was keeping the boat afloat. I've felt Jesus' presence and his grief through it all, but my own emotions didn't really start to surface until eighteen months later. It is only in this sabbatical, three years after the fact, that I've had space to process my own emotions.

"As I have been talking with Jesus in the last month or so, he is taking me back to the foundations, to something that was a core part of what shaped my walk with God very early on. It came out of the blue: 'One thing I do: forgetting what is behind and straining toward to what is ahead, I press on toward the goal' (Phil. 3:13-14 NIV). That was a foundational passage in my early walk with Jesus. For me, that passage is about knowing him experientially.

"He first spoke it to me when I was eighteen. I realized that I had a life in front of me that could be about me or with Jesus. The life I was creating didn't have a real Jesus in it, and I could see it would end in an abyss. But if I chose life with Jesus, I couldn't see where it would lead. All I could see was Jesus, extending his hand to me. I had to choose him or my own way. It was a rude awakening, because I knew a lot *about* him but didn't *know* him experientially.

"He's speaking that same word to me now. I've had so many things on my mind about the future, in a way that has been fearful and lacked hope. His word is that it is still about that one thing— not trying to figure out the past, relying on my own knowledge and experience and analysis, but about letting go. The only way to understand the past is to know him *now* and walk with him into the unknown future. That's where the focus needs to be.

"Here I am at 61 and there are so many things I experienced with Jesus—a home, a beautiful wife and marriage—better than I could ever have pulled off on my own. I was single until I was 34 and that was okay with me. I wanted to live and die in Nigeria. I never wanted the American dream. And now I've just lost all of that stuff. There is no savings, no retirement plan—it has all been taken away. I can't see the future. I can only see Jesus.

"My son will graduate from high school when I am 66. My wife is much younger than me. There is no map in front of me. All I know is that he's extending his hand like he did before, asking me to forget what is behind, take his hand, and press forward to what lies ahead. It is almost like I am back to where I was at eighteen. I don't know what life will look like. But he says, 'You trusted me before; will you trust me again?'

"That choice turned out better than I ever hoped for when I chose him as a teenager. So, (and here Jody began to pray, as tears rolled down his cheeks), 'Jesus, I choose you again in this moment. I trust you with my past and my future. Jesus, I would rather have a life with you than any other life.'

"And I am hearing Jesus say, 'Okay—let's go.'

"There is a legacy I wanted to pass on to my children: the adventure that my life was before I got married and they came along. I lived in the unknown, the possibilities—anything could happen!

"My two older boys are adults now, and Alain is approaching

manhood. I want them to be able to participate in that part of my journey—to leave a legacy of faith for them. This choice in front of me is actually an answer to prayer, that they could be witnesses to that life of faith now and not just hear about it from my stories about the past. Pondering this today has changed the fear in my heart into anticipation and expectation. I feel an excitement rising in me about the adventure that is ahead. God is in this, and he is meeting the desire of my heart for my family.

"This conversation is what I have been waiting for and wanting my entire sabbatical. I am coming away with a new perspective that God is at work. I'm looking forward with anticipation instead of a dread about the future. There is more for me than just surviving until the end."

Dearest Jody, My Brother,

Thank you for extending your hand to me. Thank you for choosing to know me—to really know me, and not stop at the superficial place of simply hearing about me. It has been my pleasure and privilege as well to get to know your heart through the adventures of these 60 years. I chose you before you were born, I chose you when your life was a mess at eighteen, and I choose you even more now, when you have become so dear to me. You always have been and always will be my chosen, my love, my man.

Twice now I have extended my hand to you at the turning points of your life, and both times you have chosen to grasp it. I reached out to you at times when I didn't especially look powerful or present in your life. In fact, they were times where you had plenty of reasons to curse me or cut me off. I want you to know what it means to me to be believed in—to know that our relationship is so solid that no matter what life throws at you, you won't leave. That knowledge is precious to me; so precious I bought it with my own blood.

To be chosen by you of your own free will is the only gift you can give me that I don't already have. My heart overflows with the thought of it—of experiencing true love from those who choose to love and be loved. And to choose that in your darkest hour—well, "Greater love has no man than this, that a man lay down his life for his friends." So, friend—thank you for giving me the greatest gift in the universe! All of heaven is honored by you.

There is yet one more time in life when you will face the loss of every created thing: at the death of your body. Once more you will look into a future you don't know, and see only me. Once more I will extend my hand to you—you have been well prepared to recognize it—and once more you will choose to trust, and grab hold of my hand. On that incredible day I will pull you up out of your world and into mine, where you will sit at my side, highly honored in the glory of heaven. That will be our best day and your greatest adventure! Let us as true friends look forward to that union with a high heart and bold anticipation.

You see, the essence of heaven is revealed in your choice. On earth, one must choose to love me. In heaven, there is no choice. When the fullness of my love is revealed, it is an irresistible force. There are no wrong choices in heaven for those who love me, because every road there leads to me. You are free in heaven only because you have already chosen me on earth.

That is also why those who have rejected me on earth may not enter heaven. When my glory is fully revealed there, any will that is resistant to my love is immediately overpowered and destroyed. It ceases to be a free will, so it also ceases to be human, and becomes nothing.

I have given you the gift of choosing me and me only on earth so that you will feel fully at home and fully alive in heaven. I have given you this gift so that the intimacy of our embrace in heaven might be deeper and longer and more satisfying. The greater your choice for me on earth, the greater your beauty in heaven. You are one of my favorites, and it is my will that you be honored as such. I would not have my greatest friends join me in my glory when they are in rags! No! I am extending my hand so that you will be clothed in the richest garments of heaven, and everyone there will know the greatness of our friendship.

Your anointing is meant to pass down through generations. It is seen in your temporal life, where you married late and had children at an older age. I knew that from the beginning and I have planned for it. You will not know the future of your children when I extend my hand to you for that last time, but I have prepared you by teaching you to trust even when you can't see.

Here's what you can know. That anointing is passing through you to your family and will rest on them, protect them and provide for them. Your provision for your family will not be measured in money, but in faith! To say it plainly, you will not leave many dollars behind when you come home to me. But you will leave planted in those you love a faith that actively generates provision, just as surely as a cache of triple-A bonds throws off interest (actually, a lot more sure than that). Your children will look back later in life and say, "The faith I inherited generated more and better provision for me than any amount of money ever could!" Look at your wife and tell me that I haven't provided far beyond all you ask or think! So be at peace and sleep easy. I have been a long time at work on your retirement plan, and I have plenty socked away to insure your future and that of your children.

Dear friend, the picture I gave you at eighteen of me extending my hand is a picture of your destiny. Back then it was a call to live for me. Today it is who you have become—one who follows me through faith into the great adventure of the unknown. Tomorrow it will become your legacy on earth and your crown of glory in heaven. You, brother, are my pride and joy. Follow me!

Honored to be your friend,

Jesus

The OUTCOME

"Actually, the interview itself really impacted me," Jody recalls, "and a lot of the pieces fell into place there with the questions I was asked. The perspective shift was like night and day—it really was a critical part of my journey. I was still on sabbatical, and disappointed with it. I had gotten a lot of physical rest, but hadn't found rest for my soul. If the sabbatical had ended before the interview, I would have said, 'That was a great vacation, but I didn't get what I needed from God.' But afterward, it was like that was all I needed from my sabbatical. The rest is just dessert. The difference between life being a desert and a dessert is that extra 'S'—seeing life as God sees it.

"I had thought that the best of my journey of faith was behind me, so my thinking was to capture that and pass it on to my children. My legacy would be a memoir of my past adventures with God. But he was saying 'No—the best is yet to come!' The story is still being written. He is reaching out his hand to me again, and now my children get to be a part of that adventure in real time. That is what restored hope for me. It is so much richer for them to get to be part of the story instead of just hearing stories about the past. And just talking about him reaching out his hand to me brings it all up afresh. It makes me cry all over again.

"When I was reading the story at the workshop, it sounded so much like the Jesus I knew. The story went further than the revelation I got in the interview. In terms of provision for my family and retirement, it fleshed out what that future of walking with him could look like. In the details I could see the blessing of taking the hand of a God who is good to me instead of seeing a dark unknown of hardship in the future.

"The part about him reaching out his hand to me again at my death—oh, yes! I will continue to take his hand throughout eternity. I just love that picture. His reaching out his hand is so precious and personal to me; the thought that it will continue forever touches me deeply.

"The standout characteristic of Jesus in this story—it's actually two things. No matter how long you've walked with Jesus and how many encounters you've had, there is still more of him to encounter and to know. That means it is never over for you. There is always more to come.

"And the *way* God chose to meet me was uniquely impact-ful to me. It wasn't just the words. It wasn't, 'Here's the standard message everyone gets in these times.' The way he met me—by bringing back our first real encounter—was uniquely designed just for me. It made the intimacy of taking his hand so much greater, because it was shaped by what was in our relationship and how we have related together in the past. The way he came to me makes me feel so known and seen by him.

"Because of that, I am confident that no matter how dark it may seem, there is still hope. We don't have to struggle to meet him—he will meet us."

Contact Jody at Jody@HeavensPerspective.com

Free in HEAVEN'S RULES

Trish Yoder is a superlative pastor whose call is to connect people with God, with ministry and with one another, bridging generations to bring people together. "I exist for the praise of his glory," she reflects. "God has shared his glory with me, so I am a glory bearer, created in his image, made to reflect him and be an extension of him.

"The story I want to talk about is my relationship with our daughter. When Elizabeth hit junior high, it seemed like every time we turned around she was in trouble. She was pregnant at 15. She is 24 now, and it was only a couple of weeks ago that she got off of house arrest. So there have been ten or twelve years of ups and downs. The big questions in my mind are, 'Why is she going through what she is? What have we done wrong that's led to it?' And, 'God, in what way do you want to teach me to fully embrace all she is?'

"My background is important to understanding who I am. All four of my grandparents were Amish, and my parents were Amish until I was two. Over the years they gradually moved from Amish to Amish-Mennonite to Conservative Mennonite to Mennonite. From age two to fourteen I lived in a very tight, Amish-Mennonite community that defined me. Even more so than my family, I found identity in that community. However, I actually got saved in the third grade in public school during an art class! What impacted me was how simple my teacher made it. I just had to believe in Jesus and ask him in, instead of following a bunch of rules and being good.

"I chose to leave my family's Amish-Mennonite church and go to a different one when I was fourteen. My parents were struggling to make it work there. For instance, church discipline was applied to my dad because he went to basketball games! The rules have always been important to me, but I didn't like how my dad was being hurt by them. I was hungry for God and wanted to be baptized, but if I was baptized into that church I would have to agree with and follow all their rules. I'd have to follow their rigid dress code, I couldn't go to sporting events or the fair, and no TV or radio. They were really serious about being separate from the world. I had a strong sense of integrity, wanting to do things right, so I asked my parents if I could go to a different church where I *could* actually follow all the rules.

"That was one of the times I felt most protected and cared for by my parents. I had become good friends with the pastor's daughter at the church that I wanted to go to. My parents met with the pastor and his wife and asked them if they would care for me if I went to that church. They agreed, and my parents allowed it.

"When our daughter Elizabeth was young, I got involved with helping young single moms who were in trouble. I would come alongside them and help them out by taking them shopping, helping with diapers and watching their children. Elizabeth went along with me. She wanted to be in on the crisis and the rescue. At one point one of the mothers and two of her kids died in a fire, and Elizabeth had been really involved in caring for those kids. I don't know if I helped her through that trauma very well.

"The drama started when Elizabeth was a freshman. She was a cheerleader, played softball and was a decent student. But she got in trouble with boys, and was untruthful about some things. At the start of the second semester we transferred her from public school to a small, faith-based school. She did well for a while, but the next year she started getting in trouble again. One morning, at like 5:00 a.m., I woke up to a call from a police officer who said, 'I have your daughter,' and I didn't even know she was gone! Another time I was at a staff meeting at church when she got caught shoplifting at the mall. I felt so out of control. I wondered, 'Should I just step down from my church role and be home 24/7?' But I never got a really clear answer from God on that.

"Elizabeth always loved babies, and she really wanted one. I've wondered if taking her along with me when I was working with those young mothers was a mistake. It seems like her wanting a baby led her off course in life and caused a lot of pain. Maybe she thought that having a baby would give her the attention she longed for from me. I think she was longing for emotional connection that I didn't know how to give her. Instead of connecting, I spent most of the time being upset with her. I was giving her truth, but not giving the relationship she really needed.

"In retrospect, a lot of that was about guarding my own heart. If I stayed shut down emotionally, things wouldn't totally blow up. I was guarding my heart against me exploding or her reacting to me saying too much, but I've realized that when I operate like that I am not being free.

"From the time she got pregnant, we always treated Elizabeth like the baby was hers. We wanted to empower her to be the mom. We gave her a choice between adoption or keeping the baby, and she felt like God said, 'If you are willing to do the hard things and take care of this baby, you should keep it.' We didn't argue with that.

"Elizabeth and Wyatt have lived with us for most of his life now. During that first year, she didn't ask us for a lot of help. In hindsight we wish we would have offered more. Maybe being so clear that she was responsible prevented her from asking us for it. And as time went on I think she needed more freedom, and that desire came out in some negative ways. There were times Wyatt would cry in the night and Elizabeth would be gone, and we wouldn't even know where she was. Immediately I'd feel the fear, and anger, too. 'Why didn't she let us know? I don't even know if she is okay!' Sometimes I would call her and ask, 'Where are you? Wyatt is crying,' and she would get home as soon as she could. She would feel bad about it, but we didn't really solve the problem, so it didn't bring us together.

"I had a lot of anxiety over it all. I kept resisting instead of embracing what our life was like, thinking, 'This is not how it was supposed to be!' I didn't always lean in very well.

"I carried a heavy sense of responsibility from my upbringing to parent her well. That message of 'training up a child in the way he should go' was deeply ingrained in me. I had such a high expectation for her to live right. Because she was our daughter, I thought, 'She ought to know better!' Somehow I had grace for others but not for our own daughter.

"I am sad that she got a harsher version of me than most people do, but we have a good connection now. I'm still not sure that my heart has been completely broken over my focus on rules. A lot of my journey with God has been about letting go of the whole law thing I learned growing up. I have been discovering I have a Papa, a Daddy who loves me and is for me, and our relationship is not based on my behavior always being good—it is based on being valuable as his daughter. The journey has been from religion to relationship.

"For instance, during her pregnancy Elizabeth's teenage friends wanted to give her a baby shower, and I really struggled with it. I thought it would give the girls the wrong impression, that we were promoting having a baby at their age. The mindset from my past was that to reach out to my daughter when she had done something wrong was condoning that behavior. But the Lord said, 'Focus on relationship and not religion; on love and not law.'

"That journey is still going on. Maybe the question I am still hanging on to today is: 'Is it okay to compromise this far? Is it okay to just love her instead of having more boundaries?'"

Trish, my Traveler,

It's a beautiful journey we've been on, isn't it? I am honored by your presence and companionship on the way. You have truly been a great friend to me! And I am deeply honored at your obedience to leave the lifestyle of obedience as an end (the faith that you grew up with), and learn the lifestyle of love that extends beyond obedience. Another way of putting that is that I've been training you to live under the rules of heaven and let go of the rules of earth. When you get here, that will make heaven feel like home, the home of your fondest dreams—and you'll fit right in. You're going to love it!

Ever since you were a girl, you've felt that pull of heaven. You knew in your heart there was a law you could follow that would give you perfect goodness and perfect freedom all at once. You were right! I just can't wait any longer to show you, so I'm going to pull up the curtain and let you in on a bit of my big surprise.

The rules of heaven are... well, different. For instance, one of our rules up here is: "You can't do anything wrong." How's that for a rule? Or how about this one: "Love is the gravity of heaven. There is no choice possible in heaven that would pull you away from love." Our rules are ones that give you total freedom, yet you never break them. In fact, they are impossible to break! We live within the laws of our Father, the laws of perfect liberty. These laws that are not choices but realities.

It works like this: on earth, you don't choose whether to submit to gravity or not, it just is. You can't violate the law of gravity even if you try. There are no possible choices on earth that take you outside the realm of physical laws like gravity.

Love in heaven is just like gravity on earth. In heaven, you don't choose whether to love or not; that choice was already made forever in your time on earth. The inclination of your heart on earth is enshrined forever as a law of heaven. Choose love on earth, and you never have to reach for it again in heaven. It is an unbreakable choice. You will be in love with me, forever, and even the possibility of doing something wrong will no longer exist for you. Every choice you make or could possibly make will all be well-pleasing to me.

Daughter, I have been preparing you for this all your life. When as a teenager you chose to move to a church where there was both more freedom and rules you could follow, I was in that. I gave you favor with your parents (partly by leveraging the conflicts they found themselves in!) and I set out years before to help create the relationships you'd need to make that jump. It was no accident you became friends with the pastor's daughter. That one only took about 20 years of planning, but it all came together quite nicely in the end.

Do you know why I sent those young mothers into your life while your daughter was young? I saw what would come with Elizabeth, and that it would grieve your heart. I grieved for you also. So I arranged that season to prepare you—to widen your heart toward young, unprepared mothers. It was my care for you that eased the awkwardness of your situation by making you familiar and comfortable with working with mothers who were still children. It was my good will to help you there. I was teaching you the laws of heaven: that I am all good, and everything I do works out for good.

But here's a secret: I also arranged that season for your daughter. It activated her love for babies and motherhood. Even the death of the two children she had cared for helped deeply root that love in her.

Elizabeth's longing for babies and children has not destroyed her life. No! It has saved it! It is her love for her baby that brings her back from running around in the middle of the night and from the irresponsible choices her desire for freedom pushes her to make. You do not know, you do not even imagine, the choices her child saved her from, or what pain hell would have brought into her life without that bond of love to hold her back. I put that love in her heart. I put the choice before her to make the hard choice, to help her heart stay bound to love. You did well to allow her to make the choice, and to honor what I was doing in her. Keep doing that! I am the Fulfiller, and you can trust me to do this well for you.

So be grateful! Be grateful that your Father in heaven is wise enough to take even a wrong choice and make of it a beautiful thing—even to use a sin to save a life! If he can do that, is there anything that is impossible for him? This too is one of the rules of heaven: "*Love conquers everything, even sin.*" (Also, "*Father rocks it.*")

Trish, you are my pride and joy, my tournament champion, my faithful friend, my long-anticipated true love. We cheer in heaven as we watch Father's plan for you take every mistake as well as every masterpiece you make, cover them with glory, and decorate the halls of heaven with the outcome. We are for you, we are with you, and we long to welcome you to be one of us forever.

With great affection,

Your Jesus

The OUTCOME

"I am really feeling affirmed as I reread this story," Trish exults, "Just redeemed! The truth and the grace and the love in it satisfies my heart. Just looking back now from heaven's perspective I see how God is in it all and making the most of it. Even the tapestry he is weaving right now is all based on what he did in those times when it hurt.

"What was most significant to me when I first read the story was the part about redemption for Elizabeth. The idea that her longing for babies and children has saved her and not destroyed her—that is powerful and encouraging! And it was encouraging for her, too, to see who she is in her destiny. We can see how he has redeemed things up to this point, and it will only continue. My story is about how God keeps setting me free from law. But he is also doing something in her story.

"After I got this I really wanted to share it with Elizabeth, but I wasn't sure how. After the workshop I was just sitting in the sanctuary unwinding, and she called. I ended up reading it to her over the phone. It was natural and beautiful and good—a really good moment of heart connection for us. Elizabeth was in tears. We both were. She was really touched by the specific details about God's redemption in her life, and felt loved, embraced, affirmed, and brought in. I was a little bit concerned that she would hear this as 'mom is talking about me behind my back,' but she received it as everything it was meant to be. It was a very good moment for the two of us. I don't feel any more that we are not connected.

"I see much more now of how far love can go for our daughter. This letter has inspired me and even given me permission to *lavishly* love her. Right now she doesn't have the means to live on her own—she is still recovering from an accident. But we are enjoying helping her get a house and step out on her own, even though she hasn't done that before. Her confidence is growing and she is maturing, so giving her that opportunity has partly come out of the inspiration we got to love lavishly.

"The thing I've learned that I'd most want to tell people about our story is that going through really frustrating times with our daughter wasn't just about her. It was about what God wanted to do in *both* of us. And, it was about finding the beauty of relationship outside of rules. I am letting go of expectations and releasing wanting life to look a certain way, and focusing on knowing and loving the person instead. As I do that, I am more and more able to make connections based on the heart and not what things look like on the outside."

Contact Trish at Trish@HeavensPerspective.com

Chapter 7:
HEAVEN AND TIME

*"But do not ignore this one fact, beloved, that with the
Lord one day is as a thousand years, and a thousand years
as one day."*

(II Pet. 3:8 RSV)

When Jesus was on the cross, one of the criminals being crucified next to him asked, "Jesus, remember me when you come in your kingdom."

Jesus replied, "Truly I say to you, today you shall be with me in paradise."

It's a beautiful story; but also one that highlights the paradox of heaven and time. Traditionally, Christians believe Jesus descended into hell during his time in the tomb, as in the Apostles Creed. But then, how could Jesus say "today" you will be with me in paradise, when he was actually in hell that day?[1]

---

1   Others believe there was a sort of intermediate place Jesus went to, a
    pre-heaven Abraham's bosom where souls resided until they could be brought

The answer is simple: heaven is outside human time.

That's hard to get your mind around, because we've never experienced the absence of time in our whole life. So let's do a few "thought experiments" to try to envision it.

On earth we live within the "arrow of time"—a term scientists use to explain the fact that time only goes in one direction. We experience each moment of time only once. In the three spatial dimensions we inhabit (up and down, side to side, and forward and back—remember those x, y, and z axes in Junior High?) we are free to run and jump and move around however we wish. I get to choose whether I go this way or that. But in the time dimension we are trapped: we can only experience one second and then the next and the next. We can't choose to jump forward or backward in time like we can in space.

Free IN TIME

Now imagine that you were "free" in the time dimension in the same way you are free in space: that you could walk backward and forward in time like you can walk back and forth across your lawn. When you look out your front window, you can see that whole lawn (all of time) in a single glance. You don't have to remember what parts of it used to look like in the past: you are seeing it right now. And you are free to open the front door and walk to any point you want to on your lawn whenever you feel like it.

The lawn represents your life in time—each blade of grass is a moment. Imagine if you could see every moment of your life at once, not as remembering what is past but as actually watching your whole life happen all at once, like watching a billion movies at the same time. And take it even farther: now imagine you could choose to walk over to any moment in your life, just like you can any spot on your lawn, and live that particular moment—again, not as recalling a memory but as actually, physically experiencing that moment all over again.

That would be a cool superpower! You could be having a conversation with someone on one part of the lawn, leave and

---

to heaven with Jesus. In the interest of brevity, I am going to stick with the traditional interpretation to make the same point.

walk over to talk to someone else, and when you rejoin the first conversation you discover it is still exactly where it left off, and you haven't missed a word. Wouldn't that be awesome?

Have you ever had that Sunday-afternoon feeling that the day is slipping by, and you can't enjoy it because Monday is already looming? That never happens in heaven. You have all the time in the world to enjoy the moment, without ever worrying that your time will run short. Time is an infinite commodity in heaven.

There is good biblical evidence that heaven functions something like this—outside our normal understanding of time. A day is like a thousand years to God, and a thousand years like a day. In other words, the bible states plainly that God does not experience time like we do. In fact, because time and space came into being with the universe (ask the big-bang cosmologists), and God created the universe, I believe God existed before time and outside of time. Everything for  him happens in the now. That's even in his name: *I am who I AM*. He is not God of the past or future, but lives in an eternal now. And we get to join him there.

Time PARADOXES

Letting go of our earth-bound conceptions of time neatly solves some mystifying biblical conundrums. For instance, the free will versus predestination conflict is based on a misconception of time. God does not foresee what happens in your life (which some argue would take away free will): he merely sees it all in his now, in the same way that you can look out the window and see your whole lawn all at once. From earth's perspective, you have a future and a past. But from heaven's perspective, in God's eternal now, he sees every moment of your earthly life unfold in front of him all at once.

But—and this is the really cool part—your heavenly life after death is part of his present in just the same way. In his eternal now, he sees you now seated with Christ in the heavenly places, covered in glory, as a tangible, living reality. In heaven's time, you are already in heaven, because heaven's perspective of time is like you looking out at your lawn and seeing all the blades of grass (the different moments of your life) all at once.

From within heaven's time, Father sees you choose and he sees the outcome of your choices all at once. He can be present to all of it without taking your free choice away. So even though it seems contradictory within earth's time, it is accurate to say that you are both predestined for heaven and have complete free will to choose it.

Because heaven is an eternal now, I believe that everyone gets to heaven on the same day. When you step through death into eternity, you are unshackled from earth's arrow of time and enter heaven's eternal freedom. There is no need for an artificial purgatory or 'intermediate heaven' to fill up the time before Jesus returns. According to heaven's clocks, everyone dies and meets him in paradise on the same day, although on earth those deaths may span thousands of years of earth time.

And here's another twist: because of this quality of heaven's time, Jesus can give you his full attention every moment for the rest of eternity, and at the same time give full attention every other denizen of heaven. Heaven's time is pretty awesome!

Mothers IN HEAVEN

"For this reason I bow my knees before the Father, from whom every family in heaven and on earth derives its name…" (Eph. 3:14-15).

Leah is a 32-year-old mother with a call to "demonstrate the power of Jesus in healing, salvation, and the whole gamut of how he brings wholeness and freedom to his people." And one of her chief instruments to advance that call is the power of vulnerability.

"My desire was always to create freedom for others. I wanted to do counseling or life coaching as a ministry, but being a strong, "D" woman wasn't always acceptable in church. Every time I would view things differently, it was always seen as threatening. So I was trying to work full-time and be a mom, and then also find places to do ministry on the side. My working mom's life was one of never-ending responsibilities and constant stress. Between ministry, child, husband, home, and my job, something in my life was always getting the short end of the stick. I felt like I couldn't do anything well. My prayer in that season was just for it to end: for relief. I wanted to be a stay-at-home mom, but with all that was going on I didn't know how to even begin to pursue what was in my heart to do with my life.

"I was pregnant with my second child at the time, and at 23 weeks I began having these odd pains. I went to the hospital three different times in one week, telling them I was in pain, but they didn't do any tests. They just said, 'You are fine,' when I knew in my gut that something was really wrong. I felt treated like a hysterical, hormonal woman—no one would listen to what I was saying.

"The third time in went in I felt like I was going into labor. They confidently assured me my contractions weren't close together enough to be the real thing, but finally, after three hours in the hospital where they kept getting stronger and closer together, they admitted they were wrong. But the drugs they gave me to stop the labor weren't working. The contractions kept building, so I asked the nurse about how long it would be until the drugs took effect. She just looked at her monitor and said, 'Well, I guess we're having a baby today!' and then walked out of the room.

"That info was like a punch in the gut—I knew 23 weeks was too soon. They took me into another room and a doctor told me it was unlikely that my child would survive. He explained that there were shots that could be given to save a premature child—but by then it was already too late to give them. And by then I was ready to push.

"As soon as Hunter was born they took him away—I didn't get to hold him or even look at him. He was only a pound and a half. It was three hours before they felt it was safe for me to get out of bed and see him. They sent me home a few hours later, but did no tests on me to determine why I had gone into labor or what the problem was.

"The doctors revived him four times that night, but about 4:30 am they called and said, 'You need to come, he will not survive another resuscitation.' As we were pulling into the hospital they called again and told me he had passed. I never had a chance to hold my son before he died.

"After the delivery I was in bad shape physically. I could hardly get out of bed or walk. At home three days later this blinding pain went through my abdomen—it felt like a laser was cutting through me. I had the chills, the shakes, then sweating—it was awful. But after so many times of being told by doctors that nothing was wrong with me, I didn't have the heart to go in to the hospital again. But after about six hours of agony I couldn't take it anymore.

"The ambulance came, and my blood pressure was like 48 over 23—horrifically low. Several times it was too low for the machines in the ambulance to even read. I was hospitalized with full-blown septic shock, multiple organ failure and pneumonia. When I heard how serious it was, the first thing that came into my heart was, 'Lord, you can't! For my husband's sake—he just lost his son, he can't lose me, too!' Then I was out. I was intubated for three weeks, and I lost all memories of the first few days in the hospital. For three weeks I couldn't even see my three-year-old. They didn't want to risk letting him in. I think the only reason I survived was a miraculous work of God.

"My biggest question in all this has been, 'Why did this happen? Jesus, if you were physically here my son would have lived!' But knowing why won't fix it—I know that. I had to live in this tension between my ideals and my reality. I know from my relationship with the Lord that some amazing redemption will come out of this. But how long will it be until I see it happen? It's the same question with my destiny: 'How long until we can walk in the fullness of our hearts' desire?' Our hearts ache to be in full-time ministry together, but I'm not seeing a lot of breakthrough in that area right now.

"In this season I've experienced first-hand some of the beautiful-ugly of life. It's been a season of really trusting in God's goodness when my reality doesn't seem to match. Trusting that his heart is for me—that he didn't do this to me.

"Part of what got me through it was a great group of people from our church surrounding me. They didn't try to explain the suffering away or say it was God's will—they were very good at just being present for us. They weren't offended by me expressing my pain to God or asking him the question on my heart: 'I felt like I trusted you, and then this happened! Are you *really* all that you say you are?' Acknowledging the reality of my current circumstances but not allowing them to define my relationship with God—I've had to fight for that, to I trust even though I don't understand.

"I'm really grateful for my husband, for his sticking with me. He has not withdrawn, but come toward me all the more. And God was so close and so comforting during that time. I got to know him truly as a Papa, where I could crawl up in his lap and he would hold me and let me cry. He kept my hope alive, even through all the tests and diagnoses and things the doctors were saying. We talked about other people in the bible who faced huge loss, like Job. And he's let me know he can handle my emotions—that emotions are okay. I can cry if I need to cry, and he's good with that. It has built in me a new ability to be honest with God about what is going on in me.

"And he has given me a picture several times of Hunter in his arms—that he's got him. That gives me hope because I will get to see Hunter again. A mother just wants to know her child is taken care of. That picture gives me hope, security and peace—this portion we have on earth is so short-lived compared with eternity.

"I have found some healing over the last few months, and I'm beginning to feel like myself again. There is redemption in the journey of doing ministry courses to get licensed. It's been a 90-degree turn in my life. But I'm still rehabbing from that illness, especially from the muscle atrophy, and I still have surgeries coming up for it.

"There are medical questions that affect my future, like whether I can have children any more. They told me there was a strong possibility that all the radiation I had in all the scans had made me infertile. The Lord has given me the promise of more children, in several different ways, but there is still probably a lot of fear in me about my health. I'm still spending a fair amount of time in the hands of doctors, and still learning to trust that they will take care of me. Putting myself back into their hands after all that happened is difficult.

"All that has been lost has allowed me to go in a direction I've always wanted—to get credentialed as a pastor. While I was in the hospital, I lost my job. I had this moment of gratefulness, though, that they had given me this huge gift: the gift of time to pursue something my heart really wanted. I have always had a heart for helping people find Jesus in the midst of their disappointments, but with everything I had going on, that dream always got put on the back burner. Now I'm headed in a direction I never thought I'd have the time to pursue. And I get quality time with my child now that I am not working! That change has been so welcome. I'm enjoying my life, just living day to day.

"But that doesn't make the grieving less. With all the beauty and the redemption, I am never going to not want my son. Even if I have fifteen other kids I will still miss Hunter. He's good—he's in the best place he could be, but I'm missing out on him being part of our family."

My Darling Leah;

Can I share a joke with you? It's the Joseph joke. The time he most despaired of ever fulfilling his destiny, when the butler and the baker had forgotten about him and he felt forgotten by me, was the moment when his releasing was right around the corner. I laugh every time it happens! No one ever sees the joke coming—what a hoot! Up here in heaven, we are all watching everything converge, seeing the pieces move together to bring fulfillment and just bursting with anticipation at as Father grabs the corner of the cloth to yank it off and reveal the masterpiece that is a person's destiny. And meanwhile on earth, that person is down in the dumps, wondering if their dreams will ever come and if we even notice them. The contrast is a never-ending source of amusement up here.

You are perfectly on course, Leah. In fact, events of late have accelerated the timetable for your destiny. The biggest preparation work you need for your calling is to grow in trust. These last six months have been an upper-level course in trusting me. And guess what? Your son played a part of that work, and so he now shares in the reward of your destiny. Hunter is going to laugh when you get to heaven, and say, "Do you see it now, mom? In only 20 hours, I pushed you several years closer to your dream! How about that for ministry effectiveness? You owe me big time!"

Walking through this situation has greatly expanded your ability to trust me. You have done extremely well. You already know this, but I never send illness or death. But I stepped in to redeem it in your life to move you years closer to your dream. Out of the pain of the death of one dream, I birthed the fulfillment of another.

But let me share this secret with you: the first dream has not died, either, because heaven does not abolish family. As Paul says, "I bow my knees before the Father, from whom every family in heaven and on earth is named…" You will be reunited as a family in heaven, as part of the greater family of my Father and your Father.

And you will live to watch your son grow up. He will not stay 20 hours old in heaven, a baby who can't talk or walk or recognize another face. Heaven is not a place where everything stands still, but where each thing grows into the full expression of what it was meant to be. You've seen me redeem things on earth, where my power is circumscribed by free will. That's a faint shadow of the power I wield to redeem in heaven! No good thing is lost on earth that heaven will not replace with its true expression.

This will all be so, my darling, because heaven stands outside of human time. You experience separation from Hunter, and the pain of separation, because you dwell inside earthly time. Earth time can never go back or jump forward, but is only experienced one moment after another. Because of that, time has taken him out of your earthly life except in memory.

However, Hunter lives in heaven's time—and there he experiences no separation from you. See, in heaven's time, everyone gets to paradise on the same day: the Day of the Lord. You will arrive the same day as Paul, as Abraham, as Elijah—and as Hunter! Because I am the I AM, the eternal present, in my presence time does not pass, but simply is. In my time, Hunter has not experienced a single day without you!

And in the same way, you will not miss a single day of his life. In heaven, you will see him grow to manhood and rejoice in his adulthood, even while heaven's time allows you to also experience him as a child, your boy. You'll have the best of both worlds. Your desire as a mother will be fully satisfied, because heaven has the power to make all things well.

In this life, Leah, you will have trouble, and miss him, and long for your son. But be of good cheer: in the next life all that will be put right forever.

I am building trust in you in this season, but there's more—a lot more. I am teaching you Father's heart. That longing you feel for your son, to hold him and be his parent and see him grow? That is the same longing Father feels for each of his children. Fellowship with him about your shared suffering. Come into his heart, and feel his longing, and understand it, and it will transform you into a true representative of your Father in Heaven.

I am turning your heart toward the broken. Through this experience you will receive the capacity to see the unseen ones, and perceive the suffering of those I long to heal. Instead of loss making you bitter, or causing you to withdraw, I am working to build an inexhaustible well of joy in you, and a compassion that leaps from the place of healing you dwell in to meet the needs of those who have nothing and no shepherd to guide them. In this you will become like me, and reveal who I am to many. I am increasing your capacity to love without being drained. And there is more I will tell you along the way.

I also want you to understand the new thing I am doing in your generation, that you are a part of. The first generation of healers I raised up in modern times were strong, with the ability to trust me in the face of great opposition. They pioneered the new thing, and are very dear to my heart. But in making them strong to overthrow a religious culture, they were often arrogant, isolated, controlling, invulnerable—powerful on the outside, but carrying deep, unhealed wounds on the inside.

My second generation stood on their shoulders, wielding the same power to heal but in a more human container. They grew in their ability to be real, and cope with the problems of healing instead of forcing the absolutes. Not needing to stand against so much opposition, they began to become members of the community, with healthy relationship with one another.

Because of the faithfulness of these first two generations, my third generation healers grew up in an environment of healing, and no longer need the tough shell. They will have a new level of compassion, a new ability to engage the brokenness in themselves and others. They will not be isolated great men or women, functioning alone, but will work in teams, fully integrated in my community instead of standing against it. They will not control or be arrogant, but love being in my body. They will be sensitive to human emotion as well as sensitive to the move of the spirit. They will not carry deep wounds inside, because I am raising my standard for my healers to be whole in heart. And their anointing will expand to heal the whole person: physically, emotionally, psychologically, relationally, and spiritually.

I am taking your generation of healers and miracle workers to a new place, one that you have never seen before. I've prioritizing building trust in you because you will need to trust me as I take you into the unknown. We are going to go places you've never been, that there are no models for, and trusting me will give you what you need to step outside your cultural beliefs and into the new thing I am creating.

In case you haven't caught this yet, I am the one doing all this in you and for you. You need only say, "Yes!" And I am going to make it fun! If we are going to journey together, why not have a blast doing it? I will hide Easter eggs for you to find, and laugh with you about the absurdity of earth's perspective, and enjoy just sharing the simple things all along the way.

All is well, daughter! I am proud of you for who you are becoming. I am pleased with you, like a master sculptor examining his just-finished masterpiece for the first time. I long to be with you, because I like you and always will. And I look forward to enjoying this road together.

Your Destiny-Giver;

Jesus

Story OUTCOME

"That story still makes me cry every time I read it," Leah recalls. "The first thing that struck me was when it talks about Hunter laughing in heaven: 'Do you see it now mom?' and 'You owe me big time!' That's how my family actually talks to each other, so I could hear Hunter saying that. It felt really personal—it felt like him.

"The idea that Hunter will never experience separation from me because heaven is outside of time—wow! I was so busy focused on redemption here on earth that I forgot about redemption for Hunter. Thinking about how we would miss him in our family, and how he wouldn't get to grow up with his family either—knowing that he won't have to grow up with that pain was incredibly healing. It makes it a lot easier. Since that week I got the story I've been able to see visions of Hunter with Jesus, where before it hurt too much to even go there and think about him in heaven. The story gave me the freedom to go there with the Lord. And seeing glimpses of Hunter in eternity opened up a realm of closeness with him, where before he felt torn away from us.

"At the very end, when the story talks about the new generation of healers—that was like putting my whole heart on paper. This is what my heart has cried out for for years—it was such a confirming word of where I am heading. Everything inside me just lit up! And it was so helpful to see that that this dream wasn't just me. It is on the Lord's heart, and he wants it for his people and his Kingdom even more than I do.

"The biggest change of perspective for me in the story was heaven's time. Trying to wrap my mind around this idea of time not being a linear, one-moment after another thing—my brain is just not wired for that! Putting yourself outside of time, where heaven sees the end from the beginning and all of it for them is here and now—that is a challenging adventure.

"What difference did the story make? It healed a lot of the places where I was really wrestling: the fact that I didn't get to hold my son, that I was too sick to stay through the night with him while he was fighting for his life. I was trying to fight off the lie that as a mother I left him all alone. The story gave me permission to deal with that lie head on, and have Father tell me that he was with Hunter every moment because we had invited him into the pregnancy and the birth. That was super-impactful for me.

"The most important thing I have taken away from this is that God really does keep his promises, in every way, shape and form. He can really do what he says he can do. The two things I asked him for after I got out of the hospital were that I didn't want to have surgery again (I didn't) and that I wanted to be pregnant again—and I am! I am over-the-moon excited! There are no words to describe how overcome I am by God's faithfulness and his goodness to me."

Contact Leah at Leah@HeavensPerspective.com

Chapter 8:
HEAVEN, SUFFERING AND GLORY

"For this slight momentary affliction is preparing for us an eternal weight of glory beyond all comparison..."

(II Cor. 4:17 RSV)

When you envision yourself fulfilling your destiny here on earth, what will it be like? In that moment when you say, "I did it! It is finished," what will you feel and experience? Often words like exhilaration, joy, gratitude, satisfaction, and contentment come to mind.

Now, let's reframe that. At what moment in Jesus' life was he was fulfilling his earthly destiny? Put yourself into that moment—visualize it, and let yourself feel it. What do you think Jesus was feeling in that moment?

Jesus' experience at the cross is pretty different than our image of destiny fulfillment! Scripture tells us why: "for the joy set before him [in heaven] he endured the cross, despising the shame..." (Heb. 12:2 RSV). *Jesus did not view the fulfillment of his destiny as something that would happen on earth, but in heaven.* The fulfillment he looked forward to was his marriage to his bride, not the sacrifice that made it possible. Jesus suffered on earth for a destiny in heaven.

Strangely, in all the thousands of people I've coached or asked about destiny, I've never met anyone who said their destiny was to be a certain thing in heaven. We seem to think of destiny as something that happens in the here and now, and so our hope is directed toward something in the here and now. Scripture disagrees. As Paul says, "If for this life only we have hoped in Christ, we are of all men most to be pitied" (I Cor. 15:19 RSV).

Here's a glorious truth: your calling has its fulfillment in heaven, not on earth. Its glory there is as much greater than any earthly fulfillment as Jesus' resurrection and ascension to the right hand of God is more glorious than his being laid in a stone-cold tomb. The Christian life only makes sense from heaven's perspective. There are things you will suffer and difficulty you will endure for your call that will never be rewarded on earth.

Heaven's DIMENSIONS

However, in heaven your suffering and sacrifice are destined to be traded in for glory. Paul (who visited heaven himself) states that in heaven we will exchange the temporary "tent" or body we are living in for an "eternal building." We will not be naked or unclothed there, but "further clothed" (II Cor. 5:2-4 RSV). The words "further clothed" in Greek literally mean "to have on over"—like to have on a coat over a shirt. In other words, we won't be beings of pure spirit, but have physical bodies—bodies with capabilities beyond those on earth but which still retain the qualities that make us ourselves.

I believe heaven is a place of extra dimensions[1]. What we get to "have on over" there is a body with more dimensions than we have on earth. When Jesus left heaven, he emptied himself of his extra-dimensional qualities—taking them off like a coat—so that he could fit into our small world. When he was resurrected

---

1   *In our universe we have four: the three spatial dimensions (think of them as directions: up and down, side to side, and backward and forward) as well as a weird fourth dimension, time.*

and returned to heaven, he put those glorious capabilities back on. In his resurrection body he could still eat and drink, his scars could be touched and his disciples recognized him. He was still himself, still human. But he had additional, otherworldly abilities. He could pass through locked doors without opening them, appear and disappear at will, or defy the law of gravity by ascending to heaven.

You are destined to be resurrected in a body like Jesus has— how cool! This raises a fun question: how do you take a limited, three-dimensional human body like yours and usher it into the five or ten or fifteen dimensions of heaven, all while still keeping you recognizable as you?

Here's an analogy that will help you visualize the problem. The Mona Lisa is a 2-D painting of a woman. If we were going to make the painting into a 3-D sculpture, how would we do it? One possibility would be to just wrap the 2-D painting of Mona Lisa over some three dimensional object (say, a dog, or a fire hydrant) like a skin. Ummm… our Mona Lisa will probably get stretched beyond recognition that way. And we haven't even specified which end of the dog her face is going to be mapped onto! That's not going to work.

A better way would be to take some visual information out of the painting and *transpose* it into a third dimension. We can do that with shadows. We know instinctively that lighter parts of a painting are closer to us and darker ones are farther away. We move the shadows backward accordingly and, voila! We have a Mona Lisa sculpture that is still recognizable as the original painting but has one more dimension. In fact, our brains have learned do this automatically. Every time we look at a two-dimensional painting or photograph, we perceive it as if it were really three-dimensional.

Suffering INTO GLORY

In the same way, heaven takes our earthly suffering and converts it into a new dimension of our heavenly bodies—glory—just as we transposed Mona Lisa from a 2-D painting to a 3-D sculpture. When Scripture talks about winning glory for oneself, the word "suffering" is usually close at hand. For instance, "This slight momentary affliction is preparing for us an eternal weight of glory beyond all comparison" (II Cor. 4:17 RSV), or "Provided we suffer with him in order that we may also be glorified with him" (Rom. 8:17 RSV), or "But we do see him who was made for a little while lower than the angels, namely, Jesus, because of the suffering of death crowned with glory and honor…" (Heb. 2:9). What you have suffered and sacrificed in this life for Christ gets transposed into the glory dimension in heaven.

In heaven, we will take up space in this glory dimension, just like we exist and take up space in earth's atmosphere. We will have glory as a physical part of ourselves, just like we have hands or feet, and it will shine out from us like light through the transparent vessel of our original three dimensions. Glory shines out from every object in heaven, including the walls, the streets, the crystal sea, and the river of life. Everyone you meet in heaven will immediately see on you the glory you won through your sacrifices on earth. When you suffer for Christ, you are actually *building your future body* in heaven.

You will never know the full reward of your suffering until you reach eternity. Those in pain always ask, "Why did this happen? Why didn't you protect me?" And God rarely answers, because the answer resides in the extra dimensions of heaven. But when you enter eternity and put on the glorified body that you helped build through your sacrificial service, all suffering will finally and fully make sense. Like Dan in this next story, you will "see the fruit of the travail of [your] soul, and be satisfied" (Is. 53:11 RSV).

Hero OF HEAVEN

At 55, Dan feels his life purpose is first to continue being a learner and a disciple, and then help others be that as well. "I am called to make disciples," Dan affirms. "I am never to be stagnant, always on a journey and never satisfied. I think it comes from the joy of discovery I had when I first became a Christian and I saw that there was so much more than just going to church.

"My big wilderness experience was my first five years in Ukraine. The stress level was huge. I had to learn the language and culture and I was wondering if I'd screwed up my whole family. My big unanswered question is, 'Why was it necessary to go through all that?'

"When I first wanted to go to the mission field, God stopped me for ten years. I felt he wanted me to go and I was ready, and then he said, 'No.' It shook me up and sent me into a real searching time, wondering, 'Have I done something wrong? Is there sin in my life?'

"Now I see it as building a broader perspective. I didn't realize at first that different cultures look at Scripture different ways. My church was so legalistic and traditional that if God hadn't prepared me I wouldn't have survived on the field. I would have been legalistic and judgmental, and I would have corrected everyone. God was getting me past the black-and-white view of life to see him at work in the gray.

"I arrived in Ukraine when I was 34 with my wife Sheryl and two little girls. It was your worst nightmare. The place was so spiritually dark you felt like you were walking in a dark cloud the whole time. The phones and internet were terrible and the roads were awful. Our living situation was pretty primitive, and it seemed like someone in the family was always sick. People were stealing from us. A man was murdered right on our front doorstep, and at one point my wife was almost kidnapped. She and the girls were out walking and this drunk man grabbed her and tried to drag her away. He had to drop her hand for a second and she ran. It happened only two blocks from our house.

"The KGB listened to our phone calls and followed me everywhere. I was interrogated once for several hours when a person with us took photos near a restricted area. Another time I got home after a trip and the KGB had called, saying, 'Dan was out here at _____, and that is not a good place to be. You better tell him not to go off alone like that again.'

"Spiritually it affected you—it was constant spiritual warfare. I didn't question our call, but we were looking for just about *any* reason to leave and still save face. It wasn't a matter of not loving the people. It was the fight. It felt like every moment was a fight to survive.

"I didn't really hear a lot from God during that time. All the chaos drowned him out. It was total overload. I started having stress and heart problems, and Sheryl and I fought more than ever in our marriage, although we had a great relationship with the girls. I got to help them grow up and was home a lot, so we became very close.

"About a year in I discovered that the pastor I was working with was embezzling funds from the church. He was 32, a young and ambitious guy with a pretty good understanding of the gospel, although a legalistic one. When the Soviet Union broke up, there were about 100 people in the church, 75% of them old grandmas. He took on the pastoral role when nobody else wanted the job. He was the only one who stepped up. He'd figured out how to work within the system, often by intimidation, because that was the Russian way. The Russians say, 'We're ruled best by a strong hand,' and that's what he did. His strong personality was attractive to the younger guys, and he brought a lot of them in.

"I tried to tell the leaders about the embezzling and was told to shut up and not say anything. As time went on, I saw that he was only interested in me as a conduit to get money in from the West, and he was skimming off the top. I tried to work with him and help him, but he saw me as a threat. He had a lot of political clout in the region (things were less than pure all the way up through the denomination), so to work against him was suicide. I ended up joining forces with a couple other guys who were perceived as threats and worked around him.

"He was very much a legalist, a manipulator and very divisive. There were half a dozen deaths that came about because of the spiritual and physical pressure he applied. I'm not talking figuratively here—people actually died. There were some young guys that he really did disciple, who became faithful believers. But those were the same guys he was stealing money from! It was weird. I would ask myself, 'How can people in the church be so loyal to someone who is so evil?' I still don't know how to answer those questions.

"After a year-long furlough in our fifth year, we switched churches and moved away from that pastor when we came back. We reached a critical mass to start training a group of guys as pastors, and started planting churches all over. The sense of darkness lifted during the 'orange revolution' when the country got a new president—but cumulative prayer certainly played a part. We had over 700 people back home praying for it.

"Ten years down the road, the leaders who had told me to shut up about the embezzling found out about it from another source. One elder came to me and asked if I still had the documents showing that he was embezzling, so I gave him a copy. When that pastor realized he was unmasked, he took all the money out of the church accounts and he and the secretary were gone in a matter of hours. He went across town and planted a charismatic church that was totally the opposite theologically and practically than what he'd done before. Nobody could figure that one out.

"It took me a long time to forgive him—there is no love lost there. I was told by the head bishop of the region to forgive him, and I replied, 'I will forgive him, but I will not trust him.'

"I still don't know why all that happened. I don't know if I could even say what God was doing in it all. I had never dealt with stuff like that—never—and there was no one to talk to. I had one individual who was a sounding board back in Kansas who would let me vent, but who had no clue about what was happening. The guy from the sending agency only came around once a year. Plus, the nearest ex-pat missionary was six hours away, and HE was embezzling funds, too!

"But I am a different person because of those years in Ukraine—like night and day. I look at my dad (a very unforgiving man) and who I might have become, and shudder. Now, with such a breadth of experience, my heart is much more open. Another change is that I am actually enjoying being a pastor. The only view I had of that role in the States was a life of static, dead-end drudgery. Becoming a coach has also helped. It's been very freeing to not have to have all the answers. So all in all, I feel blessed for being able to have been there."

Dan, My Marine,

Hail, to my great soldier, who is not afraid to charge Russian guns to win my victory! Hail to the bemedaled hero, who obeys even the order he doesn't understand for love of his General! Hail to my courageous one, who has walked through the valley of the shadow of death purely on the faith that I would be with him! Heaven takes a knee, and bows in admiration of your courage, your commitment, and your character. And on the dais before my throne a Medal of Honor waits to venerate the service of one who would give everything for me.

Well done, good and faithful servant! Enter into the joy of your Master, for your sacrificial service is widely esteemed in heaven, and your reward here will be very great.

Dan, I am exceptionally proud to call you my brother. Your beauty is in how deeply you have changed to become more like me. Your power is in the depth of your obedience. And your glory is in the largeness of your sacrifice for my Kingdom. Don't ever have a doubt about the significance of your life, because you are a shining star in heaven. Don't ever question the value of your service, because the price you paid for it makes it valuable to me beyond words. A man's glory in heaven comes from what he has suffered and sacrificed in my name on earth. In heaven your glory is very great, and I am greatly glorified in it. Son, all is well, and I am very proud of you.

Now that you have returned to your homeland and the trial is behind you, I want you to see your time in Ukraine in a new light. In your first years there, to know too much was a dangerous thing. A secret agent is told only enough to accomplish his mission. Therefore, there were many things I did not reveal at the time. You were there as a conduit of prayer that rallied those from the other countries to call heaven into that city. In clearing the land, you prepared it so those that followed you could plow. You can't plow (let alone plant seed) in a field filled with stumps and boulders. Your faith and obedience provided a flash point for my power to seep in and clear the fields, so it could break out in a church planting movement five years later. My field in Ukraine was littered with stumps by the leadership in power there, and your presence provided another way, although that was a painful process for you.

One thing I've wanted you to understand is that a key reason I chose you for this mission was my desire to rescue your pastor. How my heart grieves for him and his pain! We both know the destruction he caused and the greed that ate at his heart. You were the person I placed in his life that he didn't control and couldn't touch. You were the one who held onto his integrity. Because you knew about his embezzlement yet did not join it, you were a constant reminder to him. Every time he saw you, he saw my face. He saw me in you, and knew that I knew what he had done. I was working to bring conviction to his heart while there was still time for it to change. I showed you just enough about his problem to be my face to him, and not so much as to put you and your family in further danger.

I sent you to him because he could still be saved, and because I loved him and wanted him. I sent you because I knew you had the stability and the guts to stay the course even though it was going to be very hard. And I sent you because I loved the destiny I had entrusted him with. The work and the calling he was born to do (to extend my church throughout the region) he corrupted into an extension of hell. So I assigned his destiny to you, that my word and my call would not return to me void, but would accomplish the purpose for which I sent it forth.

In doing so, the Scripture was fulfilled, that I have torn the calling out of his hand and given it to a neighbor of his who is better than him. And yet, I still love him, and would still see him honored in my Kingdom, for the sake of the part of his heart that did love me and did take a great risk in a dark time for my name. This is the love that I have for all my children, that even the prodigals I still count as sons.

I have taken pains to teach you that I work in the gray and not just the black and white so that you could understand that all my children are dear to me, even the abusers and criminals and cheats. I do not honor men for their lack of sin, but for whatever part of their hearts they do give to me, be that small or large. And know that the lengths I have gone to rescue that pastor—I would go that far and beyond for you and for your children as well as your loved ones and friends. I would do it for you without a second thought, for you are very dear to me.

And so, my exalted and noble hero, would you do me one more favor: would you love this pastor, my son, in spite of all he has done to you and to me? I do not ask you to trust him or work with him again. I know that you have done the hard work to forgive him—for that I am grateful. Yet as my elite Marine, would you go once more unto the breach for me, dear friend, once more, and turn your heart to love him as I still love him? Then your years of service to me in Ukraine will truly be complete.

I do not ask this for him only, but for you, and for myself, and for the glory of my Father's Kingdom. To love the most undeserving ones covers you in glory here in heaven, and my Father and I will be glorified in you. In that sacrificial love all of heaven will taste the sweet savor of glory shared, which is glory multiplied, eternally.

I look forward to the day you come home to me, when I will address heaven and say, "All hail, to this Hero of Heaven!"

Your brother in arms,

Jesus

The OUTCOME

"What struck me in the story," Dan muses thoughtfully, "was the perspective of the soldier image. I had never thought of me running into the guns, running into the enemy's territory. I've often told people over the years that if I could just get to heaven and hear, 'Well done good and faithful servant!' that would be enough. After all the hard work, to hear him say those words I long to hear—that was deeply satisfying.

"I don't regret going to Ukraine. I would do it all again. I don't do things for a reward. If it is the right thing, I do it. But knowing that Jesus realized how hard it is sure helps. And when you talked about the glory of a Medal of Honor waiting for me at the steps of the throne—that part was just overwhelming.

"The idea of glory was always sort of fuzzy and ephemeral to me. I believed in it, but it was hard to grasp. But it is more tangible now. This helps me see that all things work together for good. All things are going to be for his glory, even what we suffer and sacrifice in the midst of a difficult time.

"Since we went to Ukraine I've very much disliked reading the book of Job, because there was so much going on for us that was parallel to his story. But when I read this letter, it was like at the end of Job, when he didn't need answers anymore. I don't need answers anymore, either. It all became irrelevant in the glory at the end, when I saw how God was in all the details in real time. He is a good God and he is in control, and I don't have to be. Knowing why is a curiosity, but it is not important. I don't need to know, because I know him. God had a much bigger plan than mine.

"We were often accused over there of being Western spies. I knew I wasn't one, but when it was put that way in the story (that just like with a spy God doesn't reveal everything all at once) that put a lot of pieces in place for me. If I had known it all at the start I couldn't have dealt with it. He revealed it as I needed it. I had a bigger captain, who knew what the game plan was, although I certainly didn't.

"I had never seen before how much those experiences made me into an unmovable object. I became someone who was only answerable to God, who was not going to be manipulated by that pastor or anyone. I remember one time he sort of threatened me, and said, 'Dan, you should leave and not come back to the Ukraine.' I replied, 'And you need to resign as the pastor, and you need to repent.' Guess what? I came back!

"I was shocked initially when the letter said, 'I want you to love him.' My prayer since then is 'Lord, I don't feel love toward him, but I want to love him like you do.' The perspective shift I am making is that he isn't the only one that is unlovable. There are many unlovable people that God still loves, and all my life it seems like he has given me a special ability to love them.

"To sum it all up, God is good, even when we don't understand. His call is sure, and even though it may seem scary, it's worth following. The most significant thing is that I don't need to know all the answers. They are not important, because I know him. He was there the whole time, and his perspective brings purpose even to the struggle."

Contact Dan at Dan@HeavensPerspective.com

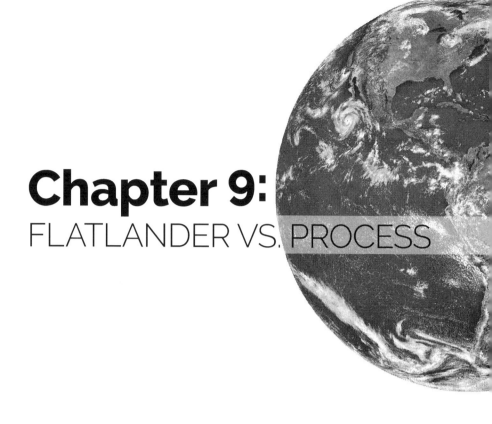

Chapter 9:
FLATLANDER VS. PROCESS

"Did you receive the Spirit by works of the law, or by hearing with faith? Are you so foolish? Having begun with the Spirit, are you now ending with the flesh?"

(Gal 3:2-3 RSV)

*F*latland: *A Romance of Many Dimensions* is the title of an obscure-but-now-influential love story published in 1884. The author imagined a world with only two dimensions—a world like a sheet of paper; a world with no up and down. The Flatlanders who lived in this horizontal realm had only two choices when they came to an obstacle: they could go left or right. There was no way over or under the obstacle, because there was no up or down in their world. Every choice they faced was a binary decision between left and right.

Most Christians are Flatlanders in the faith. When we have a decision to make (like whether to take this job, choose to witness to the cashier or give a ride to the homeless man by the side of the road) we immediately reduce it to a binary choice. For us, there is always a right decision and a wrong one. One path is in God's will is for my life, and all the others aren't. My job as a Christian is to discern God's will and choose it.

That binary thinking marks us out as Flatlanders. The Flatland we live in is called "the will of God." It's a religious belief system where in every situation God has already decided what he wants us to do. Choose right and obey, and things will go well for us. Choose wrong, and not only will things turn out badly, but we'll be disobeying God as well.

We may not believe those things theologically (in our heads), but we sure *act* like Flatlanders a lot. What can help us get in touch with how absurd that way of thinking looks to heaven? An analogy might help.

Basement DWELLERS

Imagine you have a 27-year-old son living in your basement who falls in love with a girl he met at work. He comes to you with stars in his eyes and says, "Mom, Dad, I really like this girl. But I just want to do your will. What should I do?"

"Well, son," you answer wisely, "What does your heart say? What do you want?"

"I… I surrender my will to you, Mom and Dad," he replies, gritting his teeth. "I'll submit to whatever you want. What is *your* will?"

"Well, son," you say, a bit bewildered, "You are a grown man. It's your choice who you love and who you pursue romance with."

"But, but…" he stammers. "If you would just tell me what to do here, then I'd know I am doing it right. I'm really afraid I'll blow it and mess up our relationship. I don't want to miss your best for me!"

"But son, I don't *want* to tell you who to marry. We are your parents—we'll love you just the same no matter who you choose to love. The right choice is *your* choice, not ours. Trust your heart! We trust you."

"But I just want to follow you," he continues, not even hearing. "I want all you have for me. Just tell me what you want and I'll do it."

If you were the father or mother in this conversation, what would you say next? (At least, after exclaiming, "You need be out of our basement by the end of the month!") This whole dialogue is just wrong. Not only is the son is avoiding taking responsibility for his life, *he doesn't understand what love is.* He is afraid because he believes his relationship with his parents is dependent on making the choice they want, when that isn't in their hearts at all. Love to him means obedience; but to his parents it means trust and freedom and believing in him. The son has misunderstood the fundamental goal of parenting, which is to prepare him to live as an adult who is equipped to make his own choices, not to keep him obedient for the rest of his life.

That is how Flatlander Christians relate to God. Flatlanders see themselves as children whose job is to obey and do things right, not as adults who are growing up to be peers of Jesus, into "the measure of the stature of the fullness of Christ" (chew on that phrase for a minute). Because life is about obedience, they live it as anxiously as if it were a 100,000-question multiple-choice exam where God holds the answer key and their grade determines their reward in heaven. Flatlanders believe they are loved for their obedience instead of because they are family. Consequently, they live in fear of being punished.

7 Frames

Performance	Relationship
Loss	Opportunity
Random	Destiny
Outward	Inward
Laws of Earth	Laws of Heaven
Flatlander	**Process**
Individual	Interconnected

Heaven sees things differently. Father's goal is to parent us into adulthood. It is to make us ready to marry into the Godhead, not to enforce our obedience. Our job as beloved children is to grow up into a mature bride that is a peer of Jesus—one that Father can look on and say, "Now, *that's* a catch! There's a gal I'd love to see my only son marry." We are in training to lead all of creation, because we will sit on Jesus' throne with him and rule the universe together.

So how do you train a person to lead a big organization? Give him or her *responsibility* to make decisions, manage people and handle money. When that leader masters one level of responsibility, you give him more. That is exactly how God trains us. The parable of the talents describes this process exactly.

Flatlander VS. PROCESS

The Flatlander versus Process frame helps us see life this way, as a process of growth and not simply a test of obedience. The focus is on who you are becoming through each circumstance, choice and experience. It is less about right and wrong than it is about learning to carry responsibility, and learning to make decisions together with your husband-to-be. In this view, you are being groomed to run the family business, and mistakes are part of the process. They only become failures if you fail to learn from them.

If you've walked well with Jesus for a few years, 90% of the decisions you face are not moral ones of right or wrong. You aren't deciding whether to gamble away your life savings—you are deciding between two good (or at least largely neutral) things. And here's the secret: in these choices *Jesus doesn't particularly care which option you choose!* His will is not that you pick a certain house to live in or side of the street to walk on: it is that you live and walk *together*. Father's picture of growing up is not that you become really good at obeying so that you make fewer and fewer choices of your own, but that the two of you become of one mind. Then, like the good parent of a teenager, he can more and more set you free to carry responsibility and decide, because the two of you naturally think alike.

Our images of God's will should be less like a judge, boss or general than they are a father sending his kids off to college with his blessing, or a couple planning a wedding together, or a satisfied mother watching her adult children's destinies surface in their career choices. As you read the next two stories, look for how the process mindset brings perspective to the journeys of a Flatlander.

My Beloved RULE-FOLLOWER

Courtney is a 28-year-old accountant with two young boys. Her calling is about reaching out to unchurched people in the midst of normal life—at work, in the community, and with fellow parents.

"My story is about all the times we moved when I was younger," Courtney began. "It's a long journey. It started when I was nine, and went from Wisconsin to Kansas to Oklahoma, then to New York, back to Kansas, and then to New York again, all in eight years!

"I was pretty young when we made that first move to Kansas. For a nine-year-old, it felt like a big adventure. My parents felt called by God to go and do foster care, and since I didn't have too many friends it wasn't that big of a deal to move. In foster care we had built-in friends. My parents were doing a live-in group home where two younger kids were living with us. It was a little foster-care community, four or five houses in all. We had lots of fun things to do: 4-H animals, group meals on weekends, and lots of playground equipment.

"When we moved to Oklahoma my dad took an admin role at the headquarters of the foster care agency, so we stopped having kids live with us. It really wasn't a choice on my parents' part—our location in Kansas was shutting down. That second move was harder. We went from a small, close-knit community to a much bigger one. The foster kids had come out of broken homes, so there were always some of them trying to run away or getting in trouble. That kind of thing had not been part of my growing-up experience.

"We had moved with several other families we knew from Kansas, so we had friends, but the circumstances were different for me—it was awkward time in my life. I started becoming more unsettled inside, testing my limits and figuring out who I was and what I believed in. Was I going to jump into the good crowd or the bad crowd that was there?

"Then we moved to New York. This was the part where it starts getting really difficult. We didn't have any friends there, and no built-in set of friends from foster care. We homeschooled the first semester—the public schools were huge—so we weren't making new friends at school, either. We also went to a larger, more charismatic church. We knew it was a temporary move so that dad could go to school, so I didn't spend a lot of time making friends. 'Why invest all that effort if we are just going to be gone again?' I am an introvert, so it feels like it takes a lot of energy and risk to make friends. We were in a small apartment on campus, sharing bedrooms with each other, and it was sort of embarrassing to invite friends over anyway. So my siblings and I did a lot of reading and huddling together.

"Dad was near his family in New York, so he wasn't lonely. Mom and dad had met at the college he was taking classes at, so I don't think she felt lonely, either. But I did. I am pretty introverted, but I started feeling bad about not having friends. I never really had a best friend growing up.

"During that time I started to do daily devotions. I am a rule follower by nature. I watched my parents do it and it seemed like the normal thing to do—a part of the Christian lifestyle. I had some good summer camp experiences, read Christian fiction, was in the youth group leadership, and had a lot of emotional experiences that shaped me. Those two years were sort of an immersion in the Christian culture.

"Next, we moved back to Kansas—I was fourteen now— and it was a bit like coming home. I thought we were going to be there forever. We bought a house, which made the move feel more permanent. I went back to a smaller school, and got involved in lots of extra-curricular activities. My parents' job was leading the youth group. Being involved there was a great way to connect with people. I kept busy, worked hard and did well in school, and had a lot of fun with friends. I met Skyler in youth group and we started dating in sophomore year.

"In the different places we lived I was experiencing God in different ways and environments. The church in Kansas was not as charismatic as the one in New York—not as emotional. I'd been in small communities and large groups. I'd lived with unchurched kids in foster care. And I went on mission trips for the first time. The intense encounters like the ones we had at the Navajo reservation helped me develop a heart for others.

"Then mom and dad were asked to come back to New York and be Deans at the Bible school, and they felt like God was calling them back. We took a scouting trip out there before they decided, and it was a rotten trip—I didn't want to go. Dad said to us, 'Look, we won't move if you don't want us to go.' Our response was, 'We have to do what God says.' But I asked them, 'Are you sure?' It felt like there was some doubt on their side—I wanted them to be committed.

"If God is saying this is the right decision, then I can feel secure. If it's God's call, you have to do it. You just have to accept it. But it felt like God's calling was to mom and dad and not to the family as a whole. That made it hard for me to buy into.

"So we left Kansas again when I was seventeen, right before my senior year of high school. I had to leave my boyfriend behind, and I would have been valedictorian and gotten a full-ride scholarship—one of the hardest things in moving was losing that. Skyler and I kept up a long distance relationship, so I was on the phone a lot. It was hard because we weren't able to do stuff together. He was in his first year in college and I was in a new school, so we were experiencing new things without each other. Our family moved back into an apartment again, and nothing felt settled.

"This was the first time that some doubt start to creep into my relationship with God. I thought, 'What is the deal here? Would God cause this much pain and disruption? Why would he allow this to happen?' And to myself, 'Should I even bother trying to make friends?' I didn't ever leave God, but I was very hurt and confused, and it was really hard to see him. I felt like God forgot about me, that something was happening to me that I didn't want.

"I don't know if I ever really dealt with that pain—it just sort of wore away after time. My relationship with Skyler got pretty serious, so he moved up to New York after a year and that sort of pushed the question aside. We got married and moved to Oregon six months later. I was like, 'One more move isn't going to matter.' I got a job while I was going to school full time and life became really, really busy.

"In breaks from school I cried a lot, when I wasn't distracted by life. You suppress things to get through, bottle them up to get through a busy time. Then you have a break and it all comes to the surface.

"My family had been the constant in my life through everything, and when I would allow myself to feel how much I missed them, I wondered, 'Was it a good idea to go to Oregon? Do I like my life?' I was so busy I didn't allow myself to think about what I felt or what I wanted. I would just focus on getting through the next quarter or getting through the next year. Even now it is still like that. I suppress some things.

"My kids and my husband are my family now. I've said to myself, 'I am never going to make my kids move!' I don't want my kids to go through something hard just because of our plans."

My Darling Courtney,

Before anything else, I want you to know today that I am happy with you. Never doubt that fact, because it will never change. You are a pleasure to think about.

It will be many years until the designs I set in motion through your childhood become clearly visible. I did not cause the pain of your moving—in my Kingdom, relationships never end—but I took what life gave you and shaped your destiny out of it. Your experiences with foster care exposed you first-hand to the pain the unchurched live out of, and it has given you compassion for them. You saw what it is like for them to try to fit into a Christian world, and the difficulty many Christians face in bringing them into my family. Going from smaller to larger schools and back was a similar experience, as was the challenge of making friends in new places and moving from a more charismatic church to one that was less so.

I've sensitized you to the pain of the world and the challenges of assimilation for new believers. Your desire to reach the unchurched in normal life was birthed out of these foundational experiences in moving in and out of the Christian bubble, and they are important equipment in doing it successfully. If you had always stayed in a safe Christian womb this destiny would not have been born in you.

While that is very important, I have a deeper agenda for you in this, my dear, beloved rule-follower. You have believed that if I call you to something you have to do it. But I have no orders for you that you must do. I beckon you, I lure you with affection, sometimes I challenge you—but I do not and will not control you. I am so much more interested in loving you!

When you believed you had to agree with your family's move and blindly follow orders, there was a part of that you did out of loving submission to me. I received it from you as a beautiful gift. But since that belief is not a true picture of me, it bore some bitter fruit as well. Do you see how it caused you to shy away from me, thinking I overlooked you and didn't care about how it affected you? That could never be! You are dear to me and always in my thoughts. I do not order my children around. Instead, I love to decide with you, so you feel fully a part of what we are doing together.

Thinking you know my will can give you a form of security, if your belief is that I reward you if you do things right and punish you if you don't. It gives humans a sense of control in life to think they know what will happen, and believe they can keep themselves safe in the future by following a set of rules. But that is a shallow substitute for the real thing—the security that comes from experientially knowing my bottomless love. Daughter, my will is that you find security not in following the rules, but in knowing me. Knowing what you ought to do is far, far down the list of my priorities for you. Jumping through hoops to try to please me isn't on my list at all!

Would you take my hand and walk with me in this bracing, stimulating and challenging walk of trust? Discover where you are following a rule in your life, and then ask me: "Papa, is that a rule you want me to follow? Or do you have something better?" We'll sort it out, and you'll get to know more of who I really am in the process. I will sit down with you every day like a mentor with a math student, and we will do the problems side by side. The important thing is that we'll be doing it together, not that we're solving a problem.

I am working to make you whole. Not held-together whole, not whole while you are busy enough to block out your pain—really whole. I am going to help you extract yourself from the overly-busy posture that submerges the real you. Take my hand, and join me on the journey into rest, of knowing me and knowing your-self. You don't have to fear—it will be a good journey, and I will be right there with you. Come, let's do it together!

Love always,

Jesus

The OUTCOME

"The story was really good," Courtney offered in her practical, no-nonsense way. "One of the things—mom would call this a lie I told myself—is that I have a hard time believing that God is good, and that he has good things for me even though I've had to go through difficult circumstances. I've been working lately on not having a victim mentality about it and recognizing that the challenges are a part of the journey. The end of the story where it says, *'Come, let's do it together!'*—that makes me realize that he is there with me along the way. It's a journey instead of just about getting it right.

"A couple times the story talked about my rule-following and how I focus on doing the right thing. To have some freedom from overthinking decisions, from agonizing over 'is that the right thing?'—that was a good message for me as well.

"Right at the beginning where Jesus says, 'I want you to know today that I am happy with you,' well, part of me says, '*WHY?*' It's not like I have done anything awesome in my life.

"At Bible school I saw all these people becoming pastors and going off to the mission field, when I chose to go into secular work. There is a level of guilt you feel—that you aren't really doing something with your life unless you are in full-time ministry. That's one of those things I have to work through and let Jesus speak the truth into. I am learning that he loves me no matter what and he is with me no matter what, and that it will work out no matter what.

"The idea of sitting down with God and asking if this rule is one I should follow… I feel like, a rule is a rule for a reason. If it is there for a reason, you ought to follow it. You don't really ask God about it. But maybe I need to distinguish between a real rule and one I've made for myself.

"The story was part of an awakening phase in my life—that there was something larger than just working all the time that I needed to focus on. Nothing miraculous happened as a result of that weekend, but it has been a catalyst for new kinds of thinking—and just for knowing God personally and that he is a good God.

"One thing that has been really special to me is that I was pretty sure I would never have a baby girl. My first two were boys, and Skyler's family is all boys. What I most wanted with a girl was to go look at prom dresses and do girl things with her. My mom was my best friend growing up, so I felt like I was losing my future best friend by not having any girls. But that just felt like a selfish thing for a mother to ask for. I didn't feel like I could even ask God for a girl. When I actually did have one, my dad called it an answer to prayer, and I said to myself, 'But I didn't even pray for that!' But it does feel like God being good to me and blessing me. That was really, really special.

"It is easy for a practical person like me to translate everything into 'What do I need to do?' when he is asking me just to know him. There may be a practical outcome down the road for all this, but I need to focus on knowing him first. My bottom line is just to work on knowing Jesus, knowing that he is good and knowing him for myself, not as an extension of my relationship with my parents, so that I can have my own understanding of God's goodness."

Contact Courtney at Courtney@HeavensPerspective.com

The Idol OF KNOWING

"The serpent said… 'in the day you eat from it your eyes will be opened, and you will be like God, knowing good and evil'" (Gen. 3:4-5).

Jonathan Corbin, 38, is a coach whose calling is to help leaders discover God's purpose, peace and power in their uniqueness. Asked if he could share just one message with others that he's paid a price to learn, Jonathan answers, "You can get to know God's plan for your life by learning to know the *you* that God created."

"I wouldn't say that I've experienced much suffering in life, but whenever I look back I feel the weight of the intense anxiety that plagued me," Jonathan recounts. "I was always asking myself, 'Am I doing the right thing? Am I going to be okay?' In my teen years, I'd often go on long walks on the dirt road near our house, sorting through what I was supposed to be doing in my life. I talked to God for hours, because I thought that if I did, eventually he would give me direction. God never answered me in the audible voice or vision that I wanted. Even though I never turned my back on God in belief, internally my attitude became that of the mad little kid with arms folded in a huff, who basically says, 'Fine, then I won't talk to you either!'

"My senior year of high school was a lonely, depressing time for me. I was born last, so my sister was gone and I didn't have any friends who lived close to me. That year was the first time I tried to have a relationship with a girl. I was so driven to make sure I did it right that I even asked her dad for permission to get to know her!

"Even though I was in a relationship, I felt very alone. I just wanted someone to hand me the list of expectations that I could check off to know that I was okay. I felt so much tension about it, and that made it all about getting it right and not about us getting to know each other. My conflicted feelings made me passive, and she finally ended the relationship with a talk where she said we were just friends.

"Pursuing a relationship was never casual for me. Relationship is serious. It is the first step to eventually having a family, and doing family well felt like the most important accomplishment in life. So I was really sad when it ended. I was sad that I didn't do it right and that she wouldn't take care of me. I knew I didn't do it right because it ended. I believed that if I did things right then they would turn out according to my ideal. If I could have just figured out what she needed or expected and then done that, then I would have been successful. But it didn't work, so the relationship failed and I failed.

"I needed others to be happy with me, and that meant meeting their expectations. Unconsciously, I would push people to communicate what they wanted from me so that I could come through and then experience approval from them. I was valuable if I could make others happy or maintain happy relationships. I needed others to always lead in relationships so I could know and respond to their expectations and keep things happy.

"All this really weighed on me as a hopeless feeling through my college years, into adulthood and even after I was married. On an external relational level I seemed happy. But deep inside my heart and mind that strong anxiety persisted. I would wonder, 'Why don't I have a fulfilling life? Why don't I have joy? Why would I want to invite anyone into the Christian life if it is like this?'

"My response was to keep trying. I attempted to press into my relationship with God with different prayer practices, determined that if I did enough spiritual stuff I could figure out what I really needed to accomplish with my life. But God never showed me what to *do* so that I could *know* I was doing the right thing. Once again, I felt like God didn't care about my desperate attempts to please him, so I turned back to my state of spiritual pouting. I still prayed and read my Bible, but the little kid part of me was determined to hold out until God started acting the way I wanted him to. In hindsight, I was probably clinically depressed. Everything I did or thought was tied to the question, 'Am I measuring up to people's expectations?'

"I think I got that from my family. My mom operated in that mode—constantly aware of people's expectations, and believing she was valuable because of what she did. My mom received a lot of disapproval from her mother growing up, and her main source of worth was from taking care of her younger sister. The message was, 'You are valuable if you do a good job taking care of someone else.' So in our family, that's what she did.

"Therefore, I decided early on that I was valuable if I was in a role that made *her* feel valuable. For instance, I would give her little things to do for me and then praise her for it. Or if I needed to be cared for I would tell her something I did well to get approval from her, because if she was needed to give approval she felt needed and valuable. But my world would fall apart if my mom fell apart.

"Looking back, I pretty much wanted all decisions to be made for me so I wouldn't have to be responsible. I had this powerful drive to always get back to a childhood state of freedom from responsibility. Having others decide gave me freedom from the possibility of failing, because if I can know what is expected of me, then I can fulfill it, and I will be valuable and worthy.

"I believe I am valuable when someone takes care of me, and I am valuable for what I do. That's a constant drive in my life: to put myself in a position where I am taken care of. That's what I received in my formative years and it shaped how I engaged life. Yet, through all the ups and downs and anxiety-ridden years there was something in me that wasn't going to rest until I got it figured out.

"How'd I get myself out of this trap? With lots of years of digging! It started with a business coach five years ago who helped me peel off the layers. Then I did some Theophostics (an inner healing method) and that really helped. There were things I knew in my head all my life, but this January I encountered Jesus and it became really real to me that my value and security is in that *God* values me. I can live within that and be an adult. God is taking care of things so I don't have to worry. I do have freedom to explore and figure things out.

"My biggest question about that whole season of my life in high school and college is, 'God, how could I have learned what I know now 20 years sooner?' It seems like I wasted a lot of years in anxiety to get to this point."

Jonathan, my favored son,

You know, we really like you up here, Jonathan! We get a lot of joy out of the stand-up comedy routine that is your life—watching you discover how you really look, laughing with you as you absorb the truth and change, taking pleasure in your feeling for and finding your Father in heaven. It's not just the end of health and sanctification that is pleasing to us; the process is just as much of a joy. It's like watching a baby learn to walk. No one is upset when he falls on his butt 100 times, because nothing is lost (it's not that far from your butt to the ground when you are a baby), but also because we know that you don't just magically show up one day walking. You have to learn to walk. Nothing produces good walking so much as a lot of falling on your butt.

Your life journey is a pleasure for heaven to watch, and seeing you grow is deeply satisfying. So join us, and take just as much pleasure in the journey as the destination.

The lie of your life has been that "I am valuable for what I do, so I need to do it right." It makes me happy that you have learned and are learning the truth: that you are loved, and you are valuable because you are loved. Well done! I say it again—well done, good and faithful servant!

I have a gift for you (not because you did well, but just because I like you). I want to show you some of the secret ways I worked to get you where you are today.

When you were young, you looked for rightness and security in knowing what to do. "If I can know what is expected of me," you thought, "then I can fulfill it, and I will be valuable." Knowing the right thing to do ("my will" as you humans often falsely call it) actually became an idol for you: a cheap substitute for knowing me. That was never going to satisfy your heart. Most of the prayers you prayed in those days to know my will were prayed out of fear instead of love, out of wanting to know what to do to protect your heart instead of knowing me and letting me protect you. I don't answer those fear-based prayers because I won't settle for such a shallow, pitiful solution to the cry of your heart. I didn't answer because I gave you free will and the power to decide, and when I give a gift I don't take it back. I want so much more for you that I refuse to give in to making co-dependent relationships with my children, even when it hurts my heart to not be able to give an answer.

The original sin of the human race was to substitute knowing for trusting—to take matters into your own hands and try to provide for your own deep desire for security, goodness and value by becoming wise. Adam and Eve were deceived into thinking I was holding out on them, so they chose to put their trust in the tree of knowing instead of the tree of life-connection. That didn't turn out so well, did it? So I am working to bring humanity back into the security that is your birthright—the security that is found through simple trust in your relationship with me rather than adherence to rules of performance.

On the surface, you wanted me to make the decisions for you so you wouldn't have to be responsible and risk failure. But under those prayers I saw your true desire—to be valuable. And I have responded to that longing, and I will respond to it every day for the rest of your life. Just look at you now! You know your own heart, you know me and you are wrestling yourself free from the demands of performance. All that your heart truly longed for is coming to you, my way—the free, healthy way. Everything that has happened to you over the last five years began two decades ago when you cried out to me. This is my response to those prayers.

I want you to know this: there is no shortcut that would have led you sooner to this place of knowing your own heart and knowing me. My process has unfolded perfectly in your life, according to my plan and my timing. Here's how I did it.

Phase I was to give you a taste of your destiny. I let you experience the freedom of walking fully with me early in life. Your desire to get back to your childhood experience of freedom is the key result of that first phase. I planted in you a picture of heaven that touched your true desire and became a siren call to your heart. It inoculated you against the tragedy of giving up and settling for less. Again and again in your life, that memory called you back to keep seeking the true freedom I have for you.

Phase II was to let you experience the utter uselessness of trying to find that freedom through knowledge. You had to learn that no matter how much you think through it and anticipate others' needs and try your best, it will never be enough to fill your heart's desire. There is no other way to unlearn this natural, human bent than to experience its failure.

That was a hard season, for both of us. As a Father, I longed for my son whom I saw in pain. But I knew that this slight momentary affliction was preparing you for a glory beyond comparison—the fulfillment of your true desire. It was in that hope that I let the anxiety and tension in you work its way to its natural conclusion in your teens and twenties.

When knowing what to do failed to satisfy the longing of your heart, and you were convinced that it never could, I was able to move to Phase III: knowing relationally instead of knowing rules. You came to know yourself, and me, in a much more profound way.

And son, you couldn't have done what you did in the last few years when you were 20. It was not possible! If I had tried then, your brokenness would have made every healing moment and every act of surrender into a piece of performance art done to gain my approval and give yourself value. You would have been constantly taking the temperature of our relationship, constantly looking for the signal that you were okay. All of the joy, freedom and connection of your beautiful surrender would have been lost in a wave of anxiety.

My dear son, the path I have taken you on is a good path. It is a true path, and it is the only path. There are no shortcuts for my work in your heart, because I seek more than temporary relief. I seek to fill the true desire of your heart, and fill it with myself only. Only then are you truly free, truly valuable and truly yourself.

Know this always: I am for you, I am proud of you—and I am laughing with you at the absurd beauty of your journey to becoming! Be in me, and I in you, and you will have all your desire.

My eye is always on you,

Your Father

The OUTCOME

"What grabbed me the most from the story was right at the start," Jonathan laughs, "about heaven seeing my life as a comedy routine, and the baby falling on his butt 100 times. It suddenly hit me that all my failing and all my mistakes have *no impact* on eternity. All of those failures do not affect my acceptance or my value at all. I heard heaven say, 'You are already fully accepted by me—your performance doesn't affect your value or your significance. I just love to watch you on the journey!'

"Reading it again today is really refreshing. I see so many things I have been learning over the last few years. For instance, '*Knowing the right thing to do actually became an idol for you: a cheap substitute for knowing me.*' That line really grabs me because that was what I pushed for all my life—to get it right and protect my heart. When I think that early on God was '*refusing to give in to making co-dependent relationships*' by not responding to my prayers, it gives a whole new perspective to my struggle to get God to respond to me. But he also says, '*That was a hard season, for both of us,*' which says to me that he wasn't just sitting there unfeeling, uncaring, watching me struggle. He was walking with me in that difficult process. We were connected.

"And presenting my childhood as '*a taste of [my] destiny*' transformed how I see it. I've had this theme all my life of longing to get back to my childhood state of freedom. Now, that state is no longer something that happened once and is gone, or is even something I am striving to get back, but something I am living toward. I can look forward to more and better. That really gives me hope.

"When the letter said that, '*there is no shortcut,*' part of me still says, 'Come ON! There has GOT to be a better way!' When I read, '*There is no other way to unlearn this natural, human bent than to experience its failure,*' I thought, 'Wait—there has to be another way!' That's the thing I was trying so hard to do all my life—get it right and avoid failure. Back then failure was not being valuable. But today, failure is a part of moving forward, a part of a growth process instead of a statement of who I am. That unlocks a whole bunch of freedom for continuing to grow and move forward.

"'Phase III' was a bit hard to swallow as well—that 20 years ago I would have made my surrender into *'a piece of performance art.'* If I accept that, then I have to accept who I really was back then, instead of who I *could have been* if I had gotten it right.

"See, if I think I missed it, I can still think I *could* have done it—I could have performed. So saying, 'No, actually I couldn't have done it,' means grace has to extend to who I was in the past as well as my present. I have to let go of that idealistic identity. It forces me to accept that my value even in the past is from God and not performance.

"At first I resisted that shift, but as I soaked it in (and even as I read it now) I am seeing the truth of it. It takes grace to a deeper level to look back 20 years and say, 'There is *nothing* at that point of time that would have enabled me to get it, because I would have turned it into performance.' That frees me. I know I really *am* where God can use me best right now.

"I met the God who sees and unconditionally accepts the *me* he created, the me behind the performance. When I realized he sees the real me behind all my efforts, and it has never affected the way he accepts me, the performance just melts away."

Contact Jonathan at Jonathan@HeavensPerspective.com

Chapter 10:
INDIVIDUAL VS. INTERCONNECTED

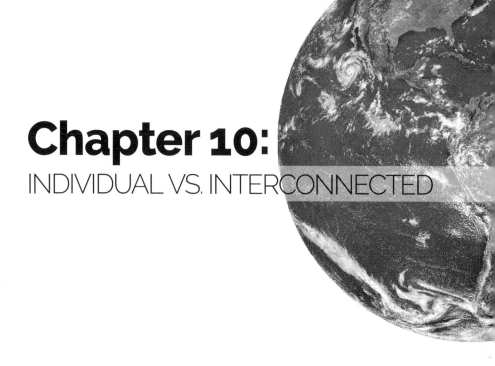

"If one member suffers, all suffer together; if one member is honored, all rejoice together."

(I Cor. 12:26 RSV)

Several years ago, I interviewed my mom, a life-long teacher, about her destiny for a book I was writing on calling (*The Calling Journey*). Sitting out on the deck in our backyard, I inquired about the life message she communicated through that role. "What was it that you wanted your students to receive through you as a teacher?"

After thinking quietly for a moment, she replied, "I always thought that my job wasn't so much to teach them as to create an environment where they could learn."

I was shocked. That was a big part of *my* destiny! I've done a ton of leadership training and curriculum design in my life, and I am constantly inserting exercises, demos, encounters, and learning games in my training, so that people learn by discovering on their own instead of being told. How did I live for almost 50 years (and write three books on life purpose discovery, no less!) and never see how much our individual destinies were interconnected?

I think now that it was the culture I was immersed in. American society is very individualistic. We define life purpose as, "What *I* am called to do with *my* life." To us, destiny is an individual, personal thing. While Eastern cultures often see it as a collective assignment to a group, for an American there is only one hero in my calling story: me.

God's LARGER STORY

There is an important truth in the American view, which is that your destiny depends on you and God alone. No person or circumstance can take it from you. But this view also misses something important; you are connected to a larger story—God's story.

Take Abraham's destiny, for instance. He was called to be the father of many nations, and to have descendants who couldn't be numbered, like the stars in the sky and sand on the seashore. That's not a calling you can accomplish in your own lifetime! His children had to have grandchildren, and the grandchildren children of their own, down through many generations, for his destiny to come to pass.

And that leads to an important insight: *his descendants' destinies were part of Abraham's destiny.* In fact, since as a Christ-follower you are a true son or daughter of Abraham, your life is also a part of the fulfillment of Abraham's calling. In heaven, you will get to run up to Abraham himself and say, "Father Abraham! Look what I have done with my life! I helped make God's dream for you come true, that because of descendants like me all the nations of the earth have been blessed through you." Abraham will wrap his arms around you like he is greeting a long-lost daughter or son, and say gratefully, "My son, my daughter, you have carried my mantle well. Since you have shared in completing my destiny, come share with me in its glory and reward."

The *Individual vs. Interconnected* frame brings this perspective into your story, that the calling you've been given is not just your own. Your life completes the destinies of many others, some of whom you do not even know. And parts of your own calling will be fulfilled through others, too. I have come to believe that *every* destiny is a shared destiny, and that Jesus planned to interconnect our lives in this way to increase the bond of love in his body. He takes the pieces of your destiny

that you do not fulfill and assigns them to others, so that when we arrive in heaven we'll find that every destiny is fully completed, and we have each other to thank for it. What a joy it will be to discover that he has covered our every mistake, that nothing he entrusted to us was lost and that we did not fall short in anything he gave us to do. In heaven, this Scripture is fulfilled:

> *"So is my word that goes out from my mouth: it will not return to me empty, but will accomplish what I desire and achieve the purpose for which I sent it" (Is. 55:11 NIV).*

Glory SHARED

This fulfillment of Father's promise will cover Jesus and his children in glory. But there's more! On earth, glory is verbal affirmation, recognition or praise. It's something one person says about another. It's also a zero-sum game. If I win the employee of the month award, you don't.

Glory in heaven is different. It is a tangible thing, a quality of who you are. As it shines out from within one, it passes into and becomes part of everyone, because we are all connected in the One God. When one is glorified, all receive the same glory. In heaven, *glory shared is glory increased.* Jesus will share his glory with us there (Rom. 5:2), and spreading it around won't leave him with less! On the contrary—we will honor him all the more for sharing it. In the same way, Jesus shares each individual destiny on earth among his body, and that doesn't diminish us. Instead, it means that everyone will receive the reward of more than one destiny in heaven.

So when the Bible tells us that "if one member is honored, all the members rejoice with it," it is saying that when it comes to honoring people, act on earth like we do in heaven. Spread the honor around and share it liberally, especially with the "unpresentable parts" who serve in the background and may not seem to deserve it.[1] Our Jesus has so much foresight he has us live like citizens of heaven now, so that when we get there we'll feel right at home. Isn't that awesome?

Your destiny is not just your own. You are part of a larger tale, God's story, and each individual calling is interconnected, woven together in the tapestry that makes up the body of Christ. As you read Andrew and Sophia's stories, let this thought penetrate your heart: that God's choice to weave our leaves together is just another vehicle for him to be good to us.

1　*These phrases are all from I Cor. 12.*

The Great TAPESTRY

Sophia, now 56, laughingly says, "I received Jesus as my Savior at ten, lost my salvation at fourteen, came back and made him Lord at sixteen, and after several years of trying and failing to be the good girl and do everything right, he became my life when I was 22. That's when the intimate relationship began, of doing life *with* him instead of *for* him. At that point nothing was working and I had to give it all to him.

"My call as I understand it now is to live life fully free and reflect this freedom to others: freedom from shame, rejection, self-doubt, disappointment—any type of bondage from the enemy. Freedom became important to me because when you've lived in the bondage, you long to get out.

"That journey started when I was fourteen. I had a wonderful life before me, and was excited about my future. I was a gymnast and did competitive downhill skiing. I was pretty free—I loved family, my parents had a great marriage, and I was looking forward to getting married and having my own family.

"One day I was out on the lake pulling my boyfriend behind the ski 'barge' he had. It was this flat thing with no guardrails or really any seats. A guy in the in the boat went to sit up front, and I yelled, 'Don't sit there—it's dangerous!' I turned to look back at my boyfriend, and when I looked forward again, the guy had done what I told him not to, fallen off the front of the boat and gotten run over. When we pulled him out of the water, his leg was almost completely severed. He survived, but my stomach was in my throat and I was shaking all over; I was so scared for him.

"The police called and I had to give them a report. A friend told me, 'His family is real litigious. You're going to get sued and your parents are going to lose everything.' My parents were awesome in the way they handled things, but to me it was devastating that I could be responsible for them losing everything. I cried and cried.

"I knew I needed to go to church the next day, and my parents went with me because they thought it would comfort me. Instead, the pastor's sermon was, 'When bad things happen to you, it proves you are not right with God and you have lost your salvation.' My parents were so upset they stood up in the middle of the service and dragged me out of church, telling me, 'We are leaving, and you are never going back.' I was bawling my eyes out as we walked down the center aisle to the back door.

"I felt completely hopeless and condemned, that this God who loved me had been ripped out of my life. All I could imagine was his face turned away from me, and that I was no longer pleasing to him. I had lost my salvation and could never get it back. I cried myself to sleep for months. That totally shut me down.

"So I went after a guy because God was unavailable to me. Before, everything had been pure, but he became my comfort, and that began to fight against my desire for purity. I got pregnant and I didn't tell anyone except my boyfriend. Then I had an abortion, so now I was a murderer. I remember thinking, 'I wish God would love me, or *someone* would love me.'

"Three years after the accident my best friend invited me to go with a group to the ocean. I found myself surrounded by grace-filled Christians, sitting around talking about stupid things they'd done that God had forgiven them for in his mercy. I interrupted, 'So you don't lose your salvation when you do bad things?' And they were like, 'No!' I remember sitting at that campfire feeling the wonder of, 'God could still love me. He could still love me!' I went home and split up with my boyfriend and said, 'I'm not going to date. I am just going to build my connection with God.'

"A few months later, that pastor got ousted from his church. He came over to our house and said, 'I realize I have severely hurt you and I am sincerely sorry. Will you forgive me?' And I told him, 'Absolutely.' That was enough at the time. But it took 20 years to really get over what happened.

"My next big struggle for freedom was in my marriage. I tried to work on my marriage for a decade, but I couldn't change my husband or fix him. I felt complete rejection there—it felt confining and controlling and there was no freedom. I was expecting this wonderful family where we did everything together, and instead I felt abandoned. I was a mess.

"Several years after we married we opened up a gas station business. I was excited about what God was going to do and how it would give us financial freedom—a place where we could actually take a vacation and still make money. Instead, it was overwhelming and all-consuming. Rather than bringing us together, it shredded our relationship because of how Fred dealt with stress. I remember thinking, 'I didn't sign up for this!' I felt like a single mom. It was extremely painful, surprising, and shocking. None of my expectations came to pass.

"I was working sixteen hours a day, plus I had a night job from 2:00 a.m. to 7:00 a.m. doing a paper route. The station was open seven days a week, and my husband couldn't let it go because of his integrity thing. He could never leave the stress. The only way he could deal with it was to numb it. Two years before we started the station, he got carpal tunnel syndrome. He couldn't work and he couldn't sleep, so his doctor told him to have a few beers at night. The pain would go away for a while, then he'd have a few more beers and go back to sleep. The drinking started as a prescription.

"My first boyfriend's dad had been an alcoholic, and I had vowed to myself I wasn't going to marry anybody who had a drinking problem. On the inside I was crying out, 'Lord, why do I have to struggle with this again when I banished alcohol from my life once before?' But we were at a church where nobody confronted anything and there was no healthy resolution. Just submit, be quiet, and don't talk about it. Fred was never abusive, but when he is in pain he withdraws and disappears. For my relational personality that is the ultimate pain.

"On our 20th anniversary in Hawaii I had a dream where I realized, 'I don't care about my husband.' I had moved to indifference because I felt so rejected—I had given up. But I had an encounter with God and I told him, 'I need to be healed and I want my marriage.' Shortly after that I was introduced to Elijah House (an inner healing ministry) and God started healing me so I could set boundaries and confront. When I started standing up for myself Fred said, 'I really liked the dumb blond.' I replied, 'She died and she is never coming back.' He didn't like it at first when I said, 'I am not going to have alcohol in our home. If you drink here I am going to leave.' He was mad for a month but he honored it.

"Looking back, that journey to freedom gave me hope, vision, compassion, and grace. I had such victory inside even though I didn't like what was happening in my family. It made me a fighter.

"Out of the blue eight months ago that pastor from my teen years got hold of me on Facebook. I was the only one he could find from his old community because of my unusual name. He said, 'I just wanted to connect with you and find out how you are doing.' When I first heard he was ministering in Japan years before, I thought, 'I hope he doesn't make a huge mess there!' But as he started sharing his story, there was a tenderness and mercy in his voice that was so different than what I had known 40 years before. He was a different man—a man of grace instead of a man of law. It was beautiful to see how he had come full circle, and for me to embrace him instead of judging him. What a joy to see the outcome of his life. He's vibrant and still doing ministry in his 80's. He and his wife have thirteen grandchildren and they have helped people go out all over the world from Japan.

"Today I have a message for anybody who is co-dependent, or whose kids are messed up, or who feels judged and distant from God. Those things that once made me feel hopeless—I know now that there is another side, there is a victory you can have in that place. He will always be there for you. I know it because he was there for me. I never thought I'd have a kid with a felony and one who was a cokehead. But the beautiful thing is, once my son had his felony, everyone felt safe to come talk to me about their struggles. So I decided to take all the stupid stuff that I did and be wide open about it so people can connect with me and I can show them compassion in their broken places."

Darling Sophia,

You are going to be so amazed when you meet me in heaven! You have done so well at meeting me in your story, and I am very proud of you, yet there is so much more you don't see. We are going to laugh and cry with joy—it will be a beautiful moment when I show you your story through heaven's eyes!

Since I just can't wait for that day, and my heart is bursting to try to hold it all in, let me give you a taste of the glory of the redemption you have waiting in heaven.

Your life and the life of that pastor who told you that you lost your salvation have been deeply connected ever since. He was a deeply religious man, struggling through his own pain to see me. His walk was like a man in a cave, groping through weeping tendrils of shame, fear and condemnation that hung from the cave's ceiling. With each step his past slimed his arms and his face, filling him with fear—a fear he expressed in control. But I loved him—deeply and passionately—and I went after him. I do not treat my people according to their condition, but according to their destiny.

The pain in him was strong enough that it took a great upheaval to redirect his life. Your life was caught in that same wave. I didn't send the upheaval—I didn't need to. His own pain produced it. That pain intruded into your life and became your pain. But in the moment when your stories became intertwined, I created a destiny of redemption for the two of you to share. Each of your lives is a thread in the great tapestry of life in heaven. But your connection is also a thread in the tapestry of my purpose.

How you engage me affects the lives of those around you. Your husband, your children and your church are all impacted by how you've pressed into my love. There is a life thread in my tapestry that binds you to them. But do you know that your prayers and your decisions affect this pastor's life in the same way his struggle did yours? It is no accident that both of you have been redeemed. Your own prayers and declarations and decisions have been a wind behind his life, and his movement toward me has been a wind behind yours. Even when you never thought of him, and through the years when you had no contact, because your stories are intertwined in heaven, your prayers are intertwined as well. The miracle of your story—that so much life and freedom were born out of your desert—isn't just a function of your decisions. It comes from the fact that you are connected in the fabric of heaven in ways you don't even realize.

Part of how I turn evil to good is allowing you to help each other unaware. That is why forgiveness is so important; it restores that life flow, turning what was a wound-connection into a life-connection. And it increases joy in heaven when what I have done is revealed, to your amazement and great delight.

Even how he contacted you a few months ago—that was me giving you a taste of heaven. It was my delight when you were born to put in your parents' hearts an unusual name, a beautiful name to me, so that he would be sure to find you 60 years later. It's just one of my pillow-chocolates for you. I enjoy those little touches of love!

When you enter into glory, you and this pastor will meet, and laugh and love. He will kneel before you, knowing truly what the fabric of heaven has accomplished in his life, and share with you the glory of all he accomplished. Every person he led to the Lord will also be credited to your account. Every spiritual child he brought to birth will be come your son or daughter, too. Every missionary he sent out will become part of your legacy.

And your glory will be shared in the same way with him. Every freedom you won and every person you touched will also be credited to him. The glory he receives in reward for his life is also yours, and your glory is also his. In heaven, sharing your glory doesn't decrease it—the one who gives and the one who receives both end up with more. In that moment, heaven will see the height of my redemption and celebrate, and see the futility of the enemy and laugh. We're laughing already!

Your life is full of intertwined connections, of people whose prayers undergird your life and who share the fruit of your victories. Fellowship and friendship on earth are a dim shadow of the connection you will experience in heaven. You're gonna love it there!

You've asked why you had to fight addictions again with your husband, when you had banished alcohol from your life in your surrender to me. (That surrender was well done—there was no defect in it.) There is no answer for why evil touches human lives the way it does, unless you wish to descend with me into hell and hear hell's twisted story. Evil is simply evil.

I rarely answer the question "Why?" because it is a question about hell. I would rather focus you on a question about heaven: "Father, how are you redeeming this to further your good purposes?" Your life has forced you to fight for freedom and it has made you a fighter. Instead of merely enjoying your own freedom, you have been forged into a weapon that brings freedom to yourself and others. That is enough for me to be very well pleased, to be overjoyed in you and who you've become! It is enough for you also. Leave behind trying to understand the purposes of evil, and be content in understanding the good purposes of your Good Father.

Sophia, I am especially fond of you. Oh, the freedom I will give you in heaven! It will be your delight to run and play and leap and bask in it. We're going to kayak over a waterfall of love and laughter—together.

Your dear friend,

Jesus

The OUTCOME

"I had never seen the impact that we have through other people from heaven's perspective," Sophia exclaims. "I never imagined that my story would impact this pastor's story. And for myself, to be part of a redemption story and have shared fruit was so encouraging. In life we bump into so many people, and the impact and influence we have is more than we can imagine.

"It motivated me to want to live and believe that for every contact and every relationship there was purpose and destiny. And hope! Such incredible hope for any relationship that goes south, that you can begin to pray for someone's destiny and be part of that transformation. It is amazing how God can take even horrific situations and turn all things to good. He is the one who sets us on that journey to hope.

"I don't live with casual relationships anymore. I live with the possibility of God working with this kind of power in every conversation, in every relationship. I don't live anymore with hopelessness because God can do this with anybody's pain. I look at people now and think, 'Lord, what do you want to be in this person's life? What do you have for them?' Before, I looked at them only in terms of what they were doing in the here and now, instead of in terms of the orchestration of heaven. Heaven's orchestration is so much bigger and broader that I can't look at anyone's life the same. Every single thing has heavenly impact.

"When I look at my son's story I see the hope of heaven at work again. I watched him change from someone brokenhearted and a prisoner of his addictions into someone whose passion is to see others fully healed of their addictions. The very thing that held him captive is the place where he has power to change other people's lives. So when I see other kids that are doing things that are destructive and painful, I start to look from heaven's perspective: what can they become and what could they accomplish if they saw how God sees them and what he wants to be in their lives? I am not hopeless anymore when I see people with addictions. Not only can they overcome them, but they can also take vengeance on the kingdom of darkness. It only takes one person to save a thousand.

"It's that ripple effect—that God is going to use everything.

How could you not be in awe of your life? He is so redemptive. He takes all the stupid things we have done and turns them around and uses them for his glory.

"The seven frames have totally changed my perspective. I've lived in them for the last few years. I used to be *performance* driven, but now I have *relationship* with God and others. Every *loss* I have I want to see as an *opportunity* to either overthrow the kingdom of hell or step into something new. I know now that nothing is *random*—that everything is part of the map that takes me to my *destiny*. Where I have overcome is where I am anointed to help others. My *inward* victory is what wins the *outward* victory for others. Now I immediately look for what *heaven* is doing in my circumstances, instead of focusing on *earth*. From the *Flatlander* analogy I learned that *process* leads to glory, so I can lean into whatever circumstance I am in instead of running from it.

"And I've learned that my *individual* story is not just about me; it is *interconnected* with everybody else's story that I come into contact with. I love that! As a high 'I' (influential personality on the DISC profile), I love to see how peoples' lives affect mine and how mine affects theirs. I'm a weaver, and I love to weave stories together."

Contact Sophia at Sophia@HeavensPerspective.com

All Your Life IS BEAUTIFUL

"I live in God's grace and acceptance as I coach, train and disciple individuals and small groups to grow to be more like Jesus." That's the calling statement of Andrew Reed, a 52-year-old pastor in Massachusetts. "And the message of my life is grace and acceptance," he affirms. "I am called to incarnate being True-faced, meaning that who I am on the outside and the inside is the same, and I am not living behind a mask or performing."

Nine years ago, Andrew entered a major transition season when his senior pastor left. He was the Executive Pastor, but had mixed feelings about being in the senior role. "I gave some push-back to God. I told him, 'You've got the wrong guy for the job.' That was the painful part of the transition. I had constructed my entire life to protect my heart, to keep myself safe from conflict and failure. That made me afraid to step into opportunities, and this was a scary one. I finally asked the elders if we could try a team leadership model. They agreed, and made me Lead Pastor.

"I thought, 'Okay, so now I am the Lead Pastor—what is that supposed to look like?' I was trying to figure out who I was expected to be in this role. 'How am I supposed to lead? What do I do?' I didn't have a clue. I wrestled with it, trying to figure out how I was going to wear so many masks at different times and please so many different people.

"I had been living behind a mask my entire life to that point, trying to be whoever people wanted me to be to win their approval and acceptance. I thought it was a good thing that I was living that way, that people liked me for my masks. For example, I so desperately craved my former senior pastor's approval that I would put on my mask of compliance whenever I went in to see him. But the longer it went on, the more I was asking, 'Is this the kind of person I want to be?' It was exhausting.

"I finally got to the place where I couldn't go on anymore. I went in for a checkup, and as I talked about the stress level I was under and how I was feeling, my doctor prescribed a test. When the results came back, he told me I had adrenal failure. 'You've lived at such a high level of stress for so many years,' he said, 'that you are no longer even producing adrenaline.' I realized, 'This isn't just affecting me emotionally, it is affecting me physically, too!'

"Things began to change when I went through a coach training program and started to process the life purpose questions in the material. The allegiance prayers[2] on control, recognition and self-image in particular were hard, where you pray things like, 'I let go of trying to control my circumstances. I let go of trying to please or impress anyone else so they will like me or approve of me. I let go of needing to be a somebody, of crafting a public image or of spinning my stories so I look better.' I saw how I tried to control situations to make others approve of me, and I thought to myself, 'I cannot pray this fully.' It gave me a picture of the depths of depravity in me. But I prayed those prayers, and told God I was giving up others' opinions, recognition, my self-image, controlling my circumstances, and trying to please people. I said, 'I want what I am saying to be true, but it isn't. Lord, make this true in my life.'

"I decided I would pray those prayers until they became true. One of the things that helped was I found key Scriptures for each area and I put personal pronouns in the verses so they spoke to me. I prayed those verses for months and months. As I chose to 'undecide' what I believed about me and to believe what God said about me instead, those prayers started to become real. I found identity in him. I saw that there was a better way and that was very motivating. It continues to motivate me to this day.

"I felt a lot of sadness as I began to tune into how I had lived my life, and in particular how I had tried to gain acceptance and love in female relationships. How pathetic it is that I operated that way! There was a lot of frustration with myself as well. I wondered, 'What could God have done if I had been fully available to him instead of being preoccupied with this false life I had constructed? Why didn't you allow me to discover this life purpose stuff earlier?'

"I guess that's my biggest unanswered question: 'What might have been?' I am asking him to restore that potential loss—what the locusts have eaten. When I think about how I parented and how I related to my wife—I did not love her well for many years—I regret living that way for so long, because it was so self-centered. I could have served God a lot better.

---

2   *From page 35 of* A Leader's Life Purpose *by Tony Stoltzfus.*

"There is this pattern where I do something I think is a failure, so I go down into the gutter until I realize that what I am feeling is not the truth of who I am. However, *Questions for Jesus* has helped me cut that response time down to next to nothing these days. I'm not sure where that belief system about failure comes from, except maybe the performance-based mentality in my family. They parented my behavior and not my heart—it was all do's and don'ts. So I read into it that approval and love come when I do the right things and when I perform well.

"My mom was raised that way. And her parents got it from their parents. She's told me that the key phrase she heard growing up was, 'What will people think?' It was all about defining yourself by the perceptions and expectations of others. Mom's siblings struggled with that, too.

"I saw myself parenting the same way, out of performance. I parented my kids' behavior, not their hearts. It was a, 'Just do what I tell you and everything will be fine,' parenting style. Now, as I am owning that, my kids and I are starting to have real conversations. My youngest son has even begun to open up about his deep desires. My wife and I have had many conversations about it, too. The change she notices is my intentionality in serving her and how much more joyful I am in doing that.

"Allowing God to shape me and not living behind a mask or trying to perform has been a long journey. I am learning to live out of God meeting my desires instead of trying to get them met by people. Ultimately, accepting the mantle of leadership at church meant accepting who I was, and what I was and wasn't called to. It's choosing to believe that I am his masterwork instead of my failings.

"Previously, I avoided conflict, because conflict was an opportunity to not be accepted. I can do it now because I don't need those in the conflict to meet my desire to be accepted. And now I'm even working with my mom to do Questions for Jesus! She wasn't brought up to ask Jesus questions and hear him speak, so it was great fun to introduce that idea to her, and see her break out of the box she has been in for so long."

Andrew,

Wow! Andrew, heaven stands in awe of your life. The way you have run to me, the changes you have made, the trust you have shown—I don't have any hesitation to show you off to heaven and say, "Look at him! This is what I am all about." My Son is planning an incredible, personalized, welcome-to-heaven party for you, with all the trappings—you're going to be blown away!

Dear son, there is one thing I long for for you: to put away your sadness and regret and embrace that all of your life is beautiful, that nothing is wasted and that all is unfolding according to my plan. Would you do me this favor, to look at your life through my eyes and see it as I see? I would be honored to show you. Here is what I see:

The performance pain has rolled down through your family for generations. Each son and daughter learned it from their parents, who learned it from their parents, and so on for years. My heart wept for them. And so I called you, as the Liberator of the Generations. Through your trust in me I have broken the curse! You said "No more!" and together we've done it—we've stopped it. In place of a curse of pain bleeding through the generations, life has begun to flow instead. Your children receive it as you own your mistakes and teach them to find their hearts' desires. Your wife receives it as you serve her well. My life even flows backward to previous generations as your mother learns to connect with my heart and my voice through your prompting. What a beautiful thing we have accomplished together!

What you must understand is that the effects of sin spanning generations are not eradicated in a day. In fact, this was a work of three generations. I planted the first seeds of this work in your grandmother decades before you were born. Her small victories passed to your mother, giving me the opening to expand the work of love in her heart in that generation. The curse they faced would not be conquered in their lifetimes. Like the prophets, they saw and greeted it from afar but couldn't fully attain it. But my plan is great enough to accomplish its purpose through the weakness of humanity. As your forerunners, your mother and grandmother have a share in your victory, and their reward in heaven will be to share fully in your reward. Every victory you achieve and every change you make will also be credited to them, because your victory was built on the foundation they laid. The change was not possible without this foundation.

You regret because you believe you could have done differently—that you could somehow have made choices that would improve on my process. You regret because you don't see the full breadth of what a change like this requires, that it began before you were even born, and so you believe it all depended on you. Son, the process of change you went through is how a curse is broken. It is the only way. There was no other path to freedom, because there was no possibility in your broken state that you could have chosen what your healed heart choses today. You could not make this change without me creating the circumstances for it. You could not make this change without the work of two generations before you.

And when my noble Liberator was finally born, I spent decades arranging circumstances to bring you to the point where this change was possible. True transformation could only happen when you grew desperately weary of living inside your masks—that desperation was the only way to give you the energy you needed to rebuild your whole identity. It took years to bring you to that point, but that is not long for me! I patiently work for years because that is what changing a human being requires.

The physical symptoms of adrenal fatigue and the words of your doctor were also a crucial part of how I was at work in you to will and to work for my good pleasure—to even want this change. You could not have truly wanted to change enough to do it without that added motivation. See how perfectly I brought that together? (I'm kind of proud of my timing on that one.)

And consider what you were learning from the Allegiance Questions and about life purpose in your coach training. Did you have that wisdom earlier in your life? Then why do you expect yourself to have acted on that wisdom before I gave it to you? Son, every change you made was a result of years of preparation on my part, and was impossible without that preparation process. There was no other choice to be made, and no other way you could have changed other than what I arranged for you.

So I say to you: "Well done, good and faithful servant! Be sad no longer, and instead enter into the joy of your master!" You have become the Liberator of

Generations. You have done all that I asked of you, in the time that I asked it. Nothing has been wasted. Nothing will be lost.

And to honor you, I myself will cover every mistake you made while I was preparing you to change. I did not ask you to change instantly, and so my part is to cover for every failure or lack on your part while my process was unfolding. Let go of believing you could have performed better. Let go and trust me to make all things well, and your letting go will release me to do it.

It is my honor, my privilege, my joy, and my desire to do this for such a noble son as you. Let us take the next step of your liberation, leave all grief and sadness behind and enter into an even deeper freedom of grace. Nothing you can do will make me happier than to let me pour grace on you until I fill up everything you have lacked.

You are deeply loved, worthy of great honor, perfectly beautiful in my eyes— you are my dear son.

With great affection,

Your Father

The OUTCOME

"When I read the story," Andrew declares, "I just kept hearing the affirmation of, 'But look how far you have come! Look at the changes we have made—and we're not done yet!' One example is the place where it says, *'one thing I long for for you: to put away your sadness and regret and embrace that* all *of your life is beautiful.'* That gave me such a sense of relief and release, to realize that I can undecide my choices to live in sadness and regret and live in redemption instead. The story granted me permission to do that. I was like, 'Ah, man, thank you! Thank you for that permission and for that release!'

"The idea that God can redeem all circumstances was so

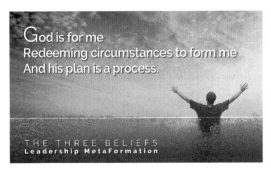

helpful to me. We talked a lot at the workshop about the Three Beliefs: that 'God is for me, redeeming circumstances to form me, and his plan is a process.' I've shared that with at least a few dozen people in the last several months. It has also been crucial to the work we do with former prisoners. They tend to ascribe everything to God by saying, 'That was God's plan!' Finally I said, 'No, that was your dumb decision!'—but God can redeem it and make something good out of it. I've used that multiple times, too.

"I loved the line *'Through your trust in me I have broken the curse! You said "No more!" and together we've done it—we've stopped it. In place of a curse of pain bleeding through the generations, life has begun to flow instead.'* That picture was a very powerful one of us working together to redeem the circumstances. My brother visited me a few weeks ago and I was able to walk him through how that pain had affected him. It had such an impact. As I laid out the Desire Discovery Cards in front of him, he was able to pick out his top desires. I asked, 'Can you think of how you are trying to get these desires met by other people?' Tears started to come as he began to realize how he was trying to get what his heart needed from others. He has lived most of his life behind a mask like I did, so to be able to share with him about what God has done for me about finding my desire in him—that was really something.

"Another spot was where the story talked about how my transformation could only come through desperation and how it takes years to change something like this. That affirmation helped me let go of the regret and the pain. That has been really big. It let me receive that I can be in this process and that God has been at work my entire life to bring me to this point.

"The part where Father talked about covering the mistakes I made while I was in process—that was very meaningful, too. I've talked to each of my adult children about this since I got the story, and I'm trusting that God can redeem even my poor parenting decisions. Just being able to release that regret is an act of trust that God will use the circumstances and use the process in their life to make them into who he wants them to be. I can still parent their hearts at this stage and speak encouragement and life to them, because now that is flowing out of my heart. Because I am in such a better place now, I can speak that life to them.

"I can see more how the life message that is in my calling statement is woven into my story—that I live in God's grace and acceptance. The idea of my name being the Liberator of Generations has been so meaningful to me, and has enabled me to get to the point where I can fully live in God's grace and acceptance."

Contact Andrew at Andrew@HeavensPerspective.com

Appendix A:
STORYWRITING RESOURCES

"Write the vision; make it plain upon tablets, so he may run who reads it. For still the vision awaits its time; it hastens to the end—it will not lie. If it seem slow, wait for it; it will surely come, it will not delay."

(Hab. 2:2-3 RSV)

Here's a brief explanation of how we created the God-stories in this book. Each individual first had a one-hour interview with a storywriter from www.HeavensPerspective.com. We asked them to tell a story that was very significant to them, included significant pain or adversity, and was one where they still had unanswered questions or weren't sure what God was doing.

Once they'd chosen a story to unpack, we asked a set of background questions (their age, personality type, calling, etc.) that helped us apply models like the Calling Journey Timeline to the story. Then, we simply had them tell their story from start to finish and asked questions along the way.

It generally takes a storywriter one to three hours to compose the God-story after the interview. The writing process relies on a combination of wisdom about the ways of God in forming us (see the list of tools below), mixed with revelation as we tune into Father's heart for the person. Out of this revelation component, we compose the stories in the first person, in the voice of Jesus or Father. Our key perspective tools are:

- **The Seven Frames** (pg. 19)
  In coaching, "reframing" is looking at something from a different point of view. The Seven Frames are seven potential ways of reframing a situation in order to see it from God's viewpoint.

- **The Bible**
  In particular, the lives of biblical characters are a great resource for learning about the dealings of God.

- **Three Beliefs** (pg. 21)
  These beliefs are: 1) God is for me; 2) redeeming circumstances to form me; and 3) and his plan is a process. These beliefs form our foundational understanding of how God works with human lives. Finding how those beliefs are operating in a life is a key part of the story-writing process.

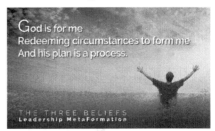

- **Formation Principles**
  These phrases capture the ways of God in working with us. For example, "You get to live the life of the people you are called to reach." This means that if you are called to reach refugees, at some point in life God will give you the opportunity to experience the refugee lifestyle. Every formation principle provides an opportunity to reframe.

- **The Desire Wheel** (pg. 16)
Our actions come from of our heart's deepest desires. The Desire Wheel (from *The Invitation* by Tony Stoltzfus) lists sixteen of the fundamental motivations God put in our hearts to draw us to him. Since God is always working to fill our desire with himself, knowing the deepest longing of a person's heart tells us a lot about what God is up to in that person's life.

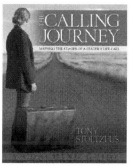

- **The Calling Journey Timeline**
The book *The Calling Journey* came out of an in-depth study of how a leader's destiny develops over a lifetime of productive seasons and valleys. Since God works differently in different stages, knowing your stage provides great perspective on what he is doing in your life. A free on-line tool for creating your calling journey timeline is located at www.TheCalling-Journey.com.

- **Personal Notes on Heaven**
These came out of insights from writing God stories, studies of Scripture and my own dialogs with Jesus (I hope to release them as a book one of these days). The more you know about heaven, the easier it is to offer heaven's perspective!

Appendix B:
GET YOUR STORY REWRITTEN

Reading your God-story can be a life-altering experience. If you'd like to receive a personal letter from Jesus like those in this book, simply visit www.HeavensPerspective.com and sign up. We'll match you with a trained storywriter, schedule your interview and start creating a special God-story just for you.

Or maybe you want to think bigger. What could happen if you gave a friend, family member, co-worker, pastor, or a missionary you know the gift of having *their* story rewritten from heaven's perspective? Gifts that really touch a person's heart are hard to find. A God-story like the ones you just read could *transform* a heart.

HeavensPerspective.com makes it easy to gift a story. Just sign up on-line, provide contact information for the person who will receive the story and we'll take care of the rest. You can even print out a gift certificate to wrap up and present as a physical gift.

Training OPPORTUNITIES

Do you want to go a step further and learn how we write heaven's stories, so that you can share heaven's perspective with your tribe? The starting point is our *Living from the Heart* work-shop (having your own story rewritten is included with your registration). This three-and-a-half day experience trains you to use the *Seven Frames* and *Three Beliefs* tools we base these God-stories on. The workshop includes plenty of practice time, so you'll gain confidence and competence to apply these tools in real-life situations.

A signature feature of each of our workshops is a 90-minute *Taste of Heaven* encounter. It uses staging, lighting, original music, actors, dance, and much more to let you experience what heaven is like. It's like no workshop you've ever attended.

To view upcoming training dates and locations, or to register, visit www.Meta-Formation.com. We would love to see you there!

Made in the USA
San Bernardino, CA
09 January 2020